2 Introductions

2a Complete the words.

1. Lisa: H_____, my name's Lisa – Lisa Grey.
2. Peter: P_____ to meet you. I'm Peter Brand.
3. James: Hi, Peter. N_____ to see you again.
4. Peter: Hello, James. H____ are you?
5. James: Very w_____, thanks. And you?
6. Peter: I'm OK, thanks. James, can I i_____ you to Lisa?
7. James: Hello Lisa. Good to m_____ you.

2b Write the phrases. Schreiben Sie die Sätze aus Teil A des Cartoons, die eine ähnliche Bedeutung haben wie die blau markierten Sätze in Aufgabe 2a, Nr. 1, 2, 3, 5 und 6.

1. _____
2. _____
3. _____
5. _____
6. _____

2c Now you: Introduce yourself.

Wählen Sie die richtige Antwort.

- [ ] 1 Oh dear!
- [ ] 2 Come in.
- [ ] 3 Nice to meet you.
- [ ] 4 Hello, Colin.
- [ ] 5 I'm ok.

3 Grammar

this, that, these, those

- **This** benutzt man für eine Person oder Sache, die nahe beim Sprecher ist.
  These ist die Mehrzahl von *this*.
- **That** benutzt man für eine weiter entfernte Person oder Sache.
  Those ist die Mehrzahl von *that*.

3a Write in the right word.

1. _____ is my colleague, Lisa Grey.
2. _____ are my friends, Mary and Jacob.
3. _____ are my neighbours, Sue and Roland.
4. Look! _____ is my teacher, Roy Young.

> **HELP**
> Diese Substantive sind in der **männlichen** und **weiblichen** Form identisch:
> *colleague* (= Kollege/Kollegin)
> *friend* (= Freund/in)
> *neighbour* (= Nachbar/in)
> *teacher* (= Lehrer/in)

4 Puzzle: The doctor's son

A man telephoned the hospital, "There's a car crash in West Street – near the bank. We need a doctor!". The doctor arrived ten minutes later and looked at the young man in the car. "Oh no," said the doctor, "that's my son!". But the doctor wasn't the young man's father. Can you explain that?

1 Step 2 | Likes and dislikes; Adjectives

1 Likes and dislikes

1a Write the phrases in the right box.

I like it. | I can't stand it. | I think it's OK. | I hate it. | I don't like it very much. | I love it. | I think it's all right. | I think it's great.

2 Say it right: Listen and repeat the sentences.

> **HELP**
> So sagen Sie, dass Sie eine Sache (Substantiv) mögen:
> *I like tennis.*
>
> So sagen Sie, dass Sie eine Aktivität (Verb) mögen:
> *I like playing tennis.*
>
> Verwenden Sie die *ing*-Form des Verbs (Gerundium) in Sätzen mit *like* und *dislike*.

1b Write about what Sarah likes and doesn't like.

1 (☺ tennis)
She

2 (☺ play - tennis)

3 (☹ watch - football)

4 (☹ swim)

3 Say it right: Listen and repeat the sentences.

2 Adjectives

2a Positive ☺ or negative ☹ ? Zeichnen Sie die passenden Gesichter.

I think it's ...

1 interesting.
2 awful.
3 great.
4 terrible.
5 nice.
6 fascinating.

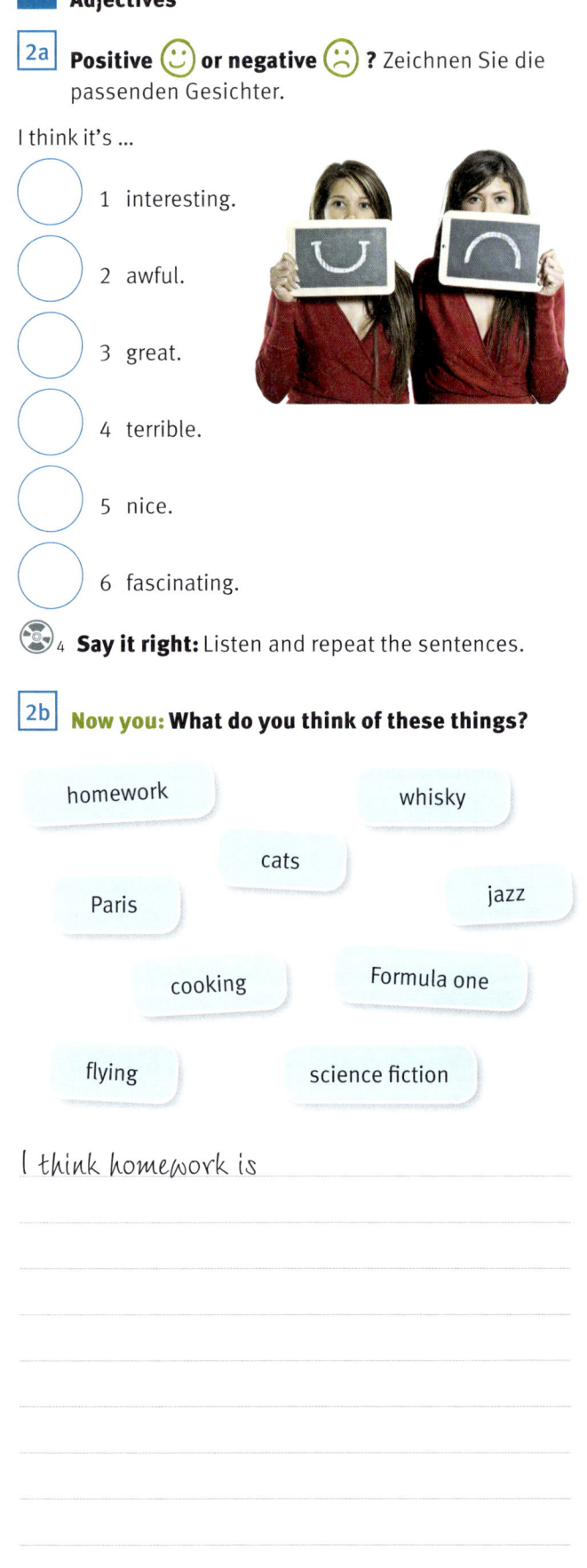

4 Say it right: Listen and repeat the sentences.

2b Now you: What do you think of these things?

homework   whisky   cats   Paris   jazz   cooking   Formula one   flying   science fiction

I think homework is

6 six 🔑 p. 52

Willkommen beim *Network Now A1 Companion*!

Mit diesem Übungsbuch können Sie die Grammatik, den Wortschatz und die Redemittel aus *Network Now A1* wiederholen und festigen. Es erwarten Sie abwechslungsreiche Übungen, interessante Lesetexte und viel Unterhaltsames. Mit der beiliegenden Audio-CD können Sie Gelerntes weiter vertiefen und Ihre Aussprache verbessern. Sie können mit Ihrem *Companion* parallel zum Kursunterricht nach jedem Step lernen oder auch nach Kursende, z. B. in den Semesterferien, um sich optimal auf den nächsten Kurs mit *Network Now A2.1* vorzubereiten.

Viel Erfolg und viel Vergnügen mit Ihrem *Network Now A1 Companion*!
Autorin und Verlag

Inhalt

Unit			Seite
Unit 1	Step 1	My name's Henry. • Sich und andere vorstellen • *this, that, these, those* • Puzzle	4
	Step 2	Über Vorlieben und Abneigungen sprechen • Adjektive • *I, my, me, etc.* • About you	6
	Step 3	Alphabet • E-Mail-Adressen richtig aussprechen • Wortschatz der Unit 1	8
	Topic	Airports	10
Unit 2	Step 1	What's the time? • Uhrzeiten • Present simple • Häufigkeitsangaben	12
	Step 2	Vorschläge machen und auf Vorschläge reagieren • Zeitangaben (*in …, on …, at …*) • What did he say? • Fragewörter	14
	Step 3	*There is / was, There are / were* • Tägliche Aktivitäten • Wortschatz der Unit 2	16
	Topic	Ireland	18
Unit 3	Step 1	Doc Martens • Past simple – regelmäßige und unregelmäßige Verben	20
	Step 2	Wettervokabular • Komplimente machen • Wörter, die man leicht verwechselt • Zeitangaben in der Vergangenheit • Über den letzten Urlaub sprechen	22
	Step 3	Jemanden einladen • Ereignisse im Leben • Wortschatz der Unit 3	24
	Topic	A get-together	26
Unit 4	Step 1	Sagen, wo sich etwas in einer Stadt befindet • *a / an, some, any* • In der Stadt • Alltagssprache	28
	Step 2	Wörter und Sätze fürs Einkaufen • Preise • *much, many, a lot of* • Puzzle	30
	Step 3	*can / can't, have to / don't have to* • Abkürzungen • Duty free shopping • Wortschatz der Unit 4	32
	Topic	Shopping	34
Unit 5	Step 1	Sätze und Wendungen fürs Telefonieren • Über Transportmittel sprechen • Amerikanisches / Britisches Englisch • Steigerung: Komparative	36
	Step 2	Steigerung: Superlative • Nach dem Weg fragen und den Weg beschreiben	38
	Step 3	Steigerung: *good* und *bad* • Sich über Verkehrsverbindungen informieren • Wortschatz der Unit 5	40
	Topic	Journeys	42
Unit 6	Step 1	Zukunft mit *going to* (1) • Zeitangaben in der Zukunft • Eine Präsentation vorbereiten	44
	Step 2	Zukunft mit *going to* (2) • New Year's resolutions • Über Zukunftspläne sprechen • Sich verabschieden	46
	Step 3	Einen Termin vereinbaren • Wiederholung der Zeiten • Wortschatz der Unit 6	48
	Topic	You	50

Key – Lösungsschlüssel 52

1 Step 1 | Reading

1 Reading: My name's Henry.

In Sydney, Australia, 120 men named Henry meet at the 'My name's Henry' convention.

Henry Pantie, from Canberra and Henry Pop, from Sydney start to fight.

Henry Jones and Henry Dyer try to stop the fight – but more Henrys start to fight! One Henry phones the police.

A policeman stops the fight. What's the policeman's name? Shane!

Glossary: meet – sich treffen | fight – streiten | try – versuchen

1a Look at Section A.
- Highlighten Sie einen Satz, mit dem Sie sich vorstellen können.
- Umkringeln Sie einen Satz, mit dem Sie jemand anderen vorstellen können.
- Unterstreichen Sie einen Satz, mit dem Sie jemanden begrüßen können, den Sie nicht kennen.
- ★Markieren Sie einen Satz, mit dem Sie jemanden begrüßen können, den Sie kennen, mit einem Sternchen.

p. 52

I, my, me, etc.; About you

3 Grammar

1	I	work in a nice office and	my	boss is very nice to	me.
2	You	work in a nice office and		boss is very nice to	you.
3	_____	works in a nice office and	his	boss is very nice to	_____.
4	She	works in a nice office and	_____	boss is very nice to	_____.
5	It	is a very nice office.	_____	windows are very big. I like	it.
6	We	work in a nice office and	_____	boss is very nice to	_____.
7	Do you	work in a nice office and is	_____	boss is nice to	_____?
8	They	don't work in a nice office and	_____	boss isn't very nice to	_____.

3a Complete the Grammar chart.

3b Song quiz: Complete the song titles.

1 Frank Sinatra:
   _____ way.

2 The Beatles:
   I want to hold _____ *hand.*

3 Abba:
   Knowing _____, *knowing*
   _____.

4 Elvis:
   _____ *can't stop loving*
   _____.

5 Queen:
   _____ *will rock*
   _____.

6 Simon & Garfunkel:
   For Emily, whenever _____ *may*
   find _____.

4 About you

4a Now you: Write about yourself.

What's your name?

Where are you from?

Where do you live?

What's your phone number?

Where do you work?

What are your hobbies?

Why do you want to speak English?

Step 3 | The alphabet; Emails

1 The alphabet

1a **Highlight the letters you find difficult.** Üben Sie die Aussprache der Buchstaben, die schwierig für Sie sind.

A B C

A rhymes with **say**
B like **to be** or not **to be**
C like **I can see** you
D like the start of **dear**
E as in **e**-mail
F say **eff**
G like the start of **jeans**
H say **eytsch**
I as in **iphone**
J like the start of **James**
K rhymes with **say**
L like the start of **elephant**
N like the start of **end**

O like **Oh dear!**
P rhymes with **see**
Q like **to queue** at the bus stop
R like **you are**
S like the start of **Estonia**
T like **a cup of tea**
U like **you are**
V like the end of **heavy**
W say **double you**
X like **ex**-husband
Y like the question word **why?**
Z say **zed** (BE) / **zie** (AE)

₅ **Say it right:** Listen and repeat.

1b **Read out the sentences.** Lesen Sie diese Sätze laut.

1 **JFK** was killed in Dallas.
2 The **RAC** is the British **ADAC**.
3 I love the film **ET**.
4 Which is better, **ZDF** or **ARD**?
5 **BBC** and **ITV** are British TV channels.
6 **m.p.h.** is *miles per hour*.
7 **VW** and **BMW** are German cars.
8 **GB** is Great Britain; **UK** is the United Kingdom.

₆ **Say it right:** Listen and repeat the sentences.

> **HELP**
>
> Sie können das **Alphabet** auf unterhaltsame Art und Weise üben:
>
> Einfach *Alphabet song* oder *ABC song* in Ihre Suchmaschine eingeben, eine Liedversion finden, die Ihnen gefällt, und mitsingen.

2 Emails

> **HELP**
>
> Letters like **THIS** are called *capital letters*.
>
> Letters like **this** are called *small letters*.

2a **Email addresses** Ordnen Sie 1–8 die richtige Aussprache zu.

1 @   a) dot
2 .   b) dot com
3 .com   c) hyphen (*or* dash)
4 www   d) underscore
5 /   e) dot co dot uk
6 .co.uk   f) at
7 -   g) slash (*or* forward slash)
8 _   h) double you double you double you

₇ **Say it right:** Listen and repeat.

2b **Country codes** Aus welchen Ländern stammen diese E-Mail-Adessen?

1 ... .gr
2 ... .ch
3 ... .pl
4 ... .at
5 ... .tr
6 ... .cz

> **HELP**
>
> Wenn Wörter in einer Internetadresse ohne Punkt hintereinander stehen, sagen Sie *'all one word'*: gamestolearnenglish.com/fast-hands = *games to learn English* **all one word** *dot com slash fast hyphen hands*.
>
> Geben Sie oben genannten Link in Ihre Suchmaschine ein und spielen Sie ein paar Vokabelspiele.

2c **Now you: Your email address**
Schreiben Sie Ihre E-Mail Adresse und üben Sie deren Aussprache.

Vocabulary from Unit 1

1 Hobbies and interests

I **play** ... tennis, the guitar, computer games.
I **go** ... skiing, shopping, to the theatre.
I'm **interested in** ... films, art, languages.
I **enjoy** ... reading, jazz, opera.

> **HELP**
> I play **the guitar**. I play **tennis**.

1a Now you: What do you do in your free time?

2 Things in a bag

2a Write the missing letters.

p__n | h__rbr__sh | p__ssp__rt | k__y |
l__pst__ck | n__wsp__p__r | c__mb

2b Now you: Write down 6 things in your bag.

3 Jobs

I'm retired / unemployed.   *Ich bin pensioniert / arbeitslos.*
I'm an optician / a housewife.   *Ich bin Augenoptiker / Hausfrau.*
I work for Siemens / a travel company.   *Ich arbeite für Siemens / eine Reisegesellschaft.*
I work in a shop / in a bank.   *Ich arbeite in einem Geschäft / in einer Bank.*

8 **Say it right:** Listen and repeat the sentences.

> **HELP**
> Verwenden Sie *a* oder *an* vor einer Berufsbezeichnung:
> *I'm **a** secretary. I'm **an** engineer.*

3a Now you: What's your job? / What do you do?

4 Form-filling

4a Match the words. Tragen Sie die Wörter ein, die eine ähnliche Bedeutung wie die Wörter im Formular haben.

family name | job | where you were born |
first name(s) | when you were born

1	Surname	....
2	Forename(s)	....
3	Place of birth	....
4	Date of birth	....
5	Occupation	....

Phrases to learn: Asking about words

Excuse me, what's this in English?   *Entschuldigung, was heißt das auf Englisch?*
What's the English word for ...?   *Wie ist das englische Wort für ...?*
How do you say ...?   *Wie sagt man ...?*
What does this mean?   *Was bedeutet das?*

9 **Say it right:** Listen and repeat the questions.

p. 52

1 Topic | Airports

1 Airport quiz
Nach welchen Personen sind diese Flughäfen benannt?

1. Munich (a politician) _____
2. Cologne/Bonn (the first German chancellor) _____
3. Salzburg (a composer) _____
4. New York City (an ex-president) _____
5. Paris (a general) _____
6. Rome (an artist) _____
7. Prague (an ex-president) _____

> **HELP**
> Machen Sie sich keine Sorgen, wenn Sie nicht jedes Wort in einem Text verstehen – häufig können Sie die Bedeutung aus dem **Kontext** erschließen. Und Sie müssen nicht jedes Wort verstehen, um die wesentlichen Informationen zu erfassen.

2 Match the biography to the right person.
Ordnen Sie dem Namen des Flughafens die passende Biografie zu.

1 ☐ John Lennon Airport, Liverpool, England

2 ☐ George Best Belfast City Airport, Northern Ireland

3 ☐ Frederico Fellini Airport, Rimini, Italy

4 ☐ Bob Hope Airport, Burbank, US

5 ☐ Tirana International Airport, Nënë Tereza, Albania

6 ☐ Ian Fleming International Airport, Boscobel, Jamaica

7 ☐ John Wayne Airport, Santa Ana, US

8 ☐ Robin Hood Airport, Doncaster, England

a) An English writer. He often worked in Jamaica – that's where he created his famous character, James Bond. He wrote twelve 007 books – and also a children's book that's now a Disney film: *Chitty Chitty Bang Bang*.

b) A British-born American comedian and film star. He hosted the Oscar ceremony 14 times and did shows for American soldiers in Vietnam. He died in 2003 when he was 100 years old!

c) A character from English history – or maybe he didn't exist! He lived in Sherwood forest with a group of outlaws. They took money from rich people and gave it to the poor.

d) This Italian film director won five Oscars. His most well-known film is *8½*. He died in 1993.

e) This American film star was born in 1907. His name was Marion Robert Morrison. He starred in 153 films – often in macho roles. Politically, he was very conservative and he worked for the Republican Party.

f) He was born in 1940 and was famous as a member of a very successful English pop group. He was murdered outside his home near New York's Central Park in 1980.

g) A footballer who played for Manchester United and the Northern Irish national team. He retired when he was 37. He loved fast cars, women and alcohol. He died in 2005 when he was 59.

h) A Roman Catholic nun. She worked with the poor in India and won the Nobel Peace Prize in 1979.

🔊 10 **Listen to the texts.**

p. 52

3 Destinations Schreiben Sie die Reiseziele in Ihrer Sprache.

Departures

Time	Destination	Flight
19:30	*Rom* — ROME	R4 4569
19:30	VENICE	EB 7134
19:40	MUNICH	DN 0045
19:45	ATHENS	OD 7156
20:00	COLOGNE	NP 4533
20:20	GENEVA	EB 7160
20:30	MILAN	R4 4581
20:30	VIENNA	NP 1976

4 Which symbol is relevant to you?

You want to …
1. find out where the Lufthansa check-in desks are. ☐ *g*
2. change some money. ☐
3. go to arrivals. ☐
4. hire a car. ☐
5. pick up your luggage at the carousel. ☐
6. go up to the next level. ☐
7. use the Internet. ☐
8. do some duty-free shopping. ☐
9. have a snack. ☐
10. meet colleagues before you get on the plane. ☐
11. phone your hotel. ☐
12. post a postcard. ☐

a)  b) c)  d)  e)  f) g) h) i) j) k) l)

Four fun facts: Airports

1 In one year, British Airways passengers eat …
- 40.5 tons of chicken
- 6 tons of caviar
- 22 tons of smoked salmon
- 557,507 boxes of chocolate

and drink …
- 81,000 litres of sparkling wine!

2 American Airlines saved $ 40,000 by taking 1 olive off every salad.

3 The world's shortest flight is the 1.5 kilometres flight from Papa Westray to Westray in the Orkney Islands, Scotland – the flight is just 96 seconds!

4 Airports with strange names: Mafia Airport in Tanzania, Batman Airport in Turkey, Danger Bay Airport in the United States, Asbestos Hill Airport and Alert Airport in Canada.

Glossary: smoked salmon – Räucherlachs | sparkling wine – Sekt | strange – merkwürdig, seltsam | bay – Bucht

2 Step 1 | Reading; Telling the time

1 Reading: What's the time?

Big Ben is London's famous icon. It's at the north end of the Houses of Parliament. But, did you know that Big Ben isn't really the name of the clock, it's the name of the bell inside the Elizabeth tower? It was probably named after the engineer who installed the bell, Sir Benjamin Hall.

The Grand Central Clock in the Grand Central Terminal, New York, is made of opal glass and is worth about 15 million dollars. It's a favourite meeting place for travellers because you can see the clock from long distances and it's directly above the station's information booth.

The Cosmo Clock 21 is a massive Ferris wheel at the Cosmo World amusement park in Yokohama, Japan. You can have a 15-minute ride on the Ferris wheel and see the sights of Yokohama from a height of 107 metres.

Glossary: bell – Glocke | tower – Turm | installed – einbaute | booth – Stand | Ferris wheel – Riesenrad | sights – Sehenswürdigkeiten | height – Höhe

🔘 11 **Listen to the texts.**

> **HELP**
> Wenn Sie jemand nach der Uhrzeit fragt, müssen Sie diese meistens nicht auf die Minute genau angeben. Ist es z. B. 24 Minuten nach eins oder 17 Minuten vor sieben, können Sie sagen: *It's **about** twenty-five past one* bzw. *It's **about** quarter to seven*.

1a What's the time in the three pictures?

1 _____
2 _____
3 _____

> **HELP**
> 6.30 (halb sieben) = half **past** six

2 Telling the time

2a What time is it?

1 12:30
2 04:25
3 07:10
4 02:45
5 04:40
6 07:55

1 It's
2
3
4
5
6

🔘 12 **Say it right:** Listen and repeat the sentences.

> **HELP**
> Die 24-Stunden-Uhrzeitangabe wird für Fahrpläne, z. B. Zugfahrpläne, verwendet. Für alle Uhrzeiten zwischen 0.00 und 11.59 gibt man *am* (= ante meridiem), für alle Uhrzeiten zwischen 12.00 und 23.59 gibt man *pm* (= post meridiem) an. Oder man sagt: *Ten o'clock **in the morning**, Three o'clock **in the afternoon**, Eleven o'clock **at night**.*

2b Write the times in two ways.

1 13.45 | 1.45 pm quarter to two in the afternoon
4 21.35
2 23.15
5 10.10
3 3.30
6 14.20

🔘 13 **Say it right:** Listen and repeat.

12 twelve   p. 52

Present simple; Adverbs of frequency

3 Grammar

Present simple

Mit dem Present simple spricht man über Dinge,
– die man regelmäßig macht: *I play tennis every week.*
oder
– die immer gelten: *I like tennis.*

1 **Do** you **like** hockey?
2 Yes, I **do**. / No, I **don't**.
3 I **like** tennis but I **don't like** hockey.

HELP
He, she, it, das **S** muss mit.

3a **Write sentences with *he*.** Verwenden Sie *he* und schreiben Sie ähnliche Sätze wie die Sätze 1–3 im Grammatikkasten oben.

1 _____
2 _____
3 _____

3b **Cross out the wrong words.**

1 **Do** | **Does** you **like** | **likes** Italian food?
2 I **do** | **does** but my husband **don't** | **doesn't**.
3 What kind of food **do** | **does** he **enjoy** | **enjoys**?
4 He **enjoy** | **enjoys** Chinese food but I **think** | **thinks** he **prefer** | **prefers** Thai.
5 **Do** | **Does** you often **go** | **goes** to restaurants?
6 No, we **don't** | **doesn't**. He **don't** | **doesn't** really **like** | **likes** to pay so much money!

3c **Now you: What do you like?**

1 Do you like Italian food?

_____

2 What's your favourite food?

_____

3 Which is your favourite restaurant?

_____

4 Grammar

Adverbs of frequency

Words of frequency: **always, usually, often, sometimes, never, ...**
Phrases of frequency: **every day, once a week, twice a month, ...**

1 I **always** arrive on time.
2 We are **never** late.
3 I go there **every week**.

☐ a) Längere Häufigkeitsangaben stehen normalerweise am Ende des Satzes.
☐ b) Kürzere Häufigkeitsangaben stehen normalerweise vor dem Verb.
☐ c) Ausnahme: Das Verb *to be (am, is, are)* – hier stehen kürzere Häufigkeitsangaben nach dem Verb.

4a **Match the sentences to the rules.** Ordnen Sie im Grammatikkasten oben die Sätze 1–3 den richtigen Regeln a)–c) zu.

4b **Now you: Answer the questions.**
Verwenden Sie eine Häufigkeitsangabe in Ihrer Antwort.

1 How often do you get up after ten am?

_____

2 How often do you go on holiday?

_____

3 How often do you eat in a restaurant?

_____

4 How often do you travel by taxi?

_____

5 How often do you play computer games?

_____

6 How often do you have an English lesson?

_____

7 How often do you do your homework?

_____

8 How often are you late for work?

_____

p. 52

Step 2 | Suggestions; Time phrases (in ..., on ..., at ...)

1 Suggestions

1a Match the halves of the sentences. Einen Kater kann man ganz unterschiedlich bekämpfen ... Welche landestypischen Tipps gibt es?

When you have a hangover, ...
1. the Japanese man suggests, *Why ...*
2. the German says, *We ...*
3. the American says, *How about ...*
4. the Russian suggests, *Let's ...*
5. the Englishman says, *Shall ...*

    a) *eat lemon with sugar and ground coffee on top.*
    b) *don't we have some fish soup?*
    c) *eating a raw egg with Tabasco, salt and pepper?*
    d) *we have a bacon sandwich?*
    e) *could eat pickled fish.*

Glossary: ground coffee – gemahlener Kaffee | raw – roh | pickled – (in Essig) eingelegt

1b Now you: Suggest a cure for a hangover.

1c Complete the suggestions.

drink | drinking | to drink

1. Shall we _____ tea?
2. Let's _____ tea.
3. Why don't you _____ tea?
4. How about _____ tea?
5. We could _____ tea.
6. Would you like _____ tea?

🔊 14 **Say it right:** Listen and repeat the sentences.

1d Complete the phrases. Ergänzen Sie die Reaktionen auf einen Vorschlag.

1. Good i_____ .   3. That s_____ great.
2. I'd l_____ to.   4. S_____ , I can't.

HELP

BE	AE
– **at** the weekend	– **on** the weekend
– 11.12 = the **eleventh** of December	– 11.12 = the **twelfth** of November

2 Time phrases (in ..., on, ..., at ...)

2a Write the time phrases in the right box.

Christmas Day | the morning | Wednesday | May | Christmas | 1952 | my birthday | 9.30 | Easter | summer | February 1st | night

IN

ON

AT

🔊 15 **Say it right:** Listen and repeat.

2b Now you: When do you ...

have a party? _____
get presents? _____
do housework? _____
go shopping? _____
have lunch? _____
watch TV? _____

p. 52

14 fourteen

Reading; Question words

3 Reading: What did he say?

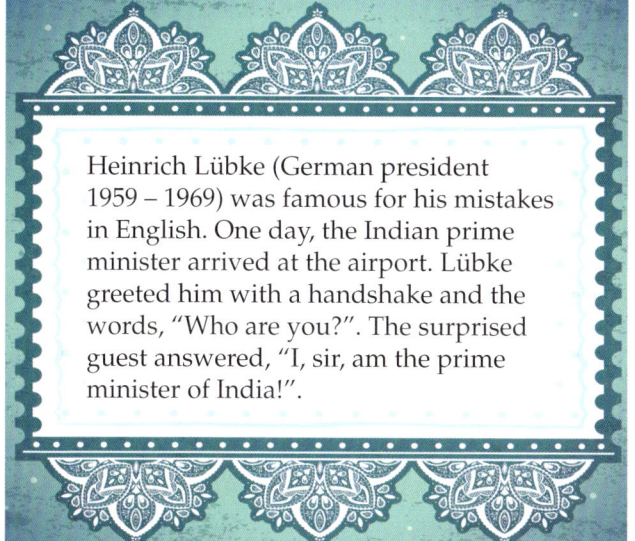

Heinrich Lübke (German president 1959 – 1969) was famous for his mistakes in English. One day, the Indian prime minister arrived at the airport. Lübke greeted him with a handshake and the words, "Who are you?". The surprised guest answered, "I, sir, am the prime minister of India!".

🔊 16 **Listen to the text.**

3a In Lübke's words …

1 What did Lübke really want to ask the prime minister?

_____

2 Which two words did Lübke confuse?

_____ / _____

4 Grammar

Question words

Who …?	Whose …?
Where …?	Which …?
When …?	Why …?
What …?	How much / often / old …?

4a Write in the question words.

1 _____ book is that? – I think it's Peter's.

2 _____ did you come to the course today? – By car.

3 _____ is your favourite actor? – Brad Pitt.

4 _____ is your suitcase? – The blue one.

5 _____ are you? – Fine, thanks.

6 _____ do you want to learn English? – Because I need it at work.

> **HELP**
> Beginnen Sie Fragen nie mit einer Präposition:
> *What are you looking **at**?*
> *What are you talking **about**?*

4b Write in the preposition.

1 Where do you come _____?
2 Which town do you live _____?
3 Which company do you work _____?
4 What kind of music do you listen _____?
5 Which sports are you interested _____?
6 Who did you write your last email _____?
7 In your last lesson, what topics did you talk _____?
8 Who was the last person you talked _____?

🔊 17 **Say it right:** Listen and repeat the questions.

4c Now you: Answer the questions in exercise 4b.

1 _____

2 _____

3 _____

4 _____

5 _____

6 _____

7 _____

8 _____

p. 52

2 Step 3 | There is / was, There are / were; Daily routines

1 Grammar

	Present	Past
Singular	There is(n't)	There was(n't)
Plural	There are(n't)	There were(n't)

1a Complete the sentences. Verwenden Sie die Ausdrücke im Grammatikkasten oben.

1 _____ a boring marketing meeting yesterday and _____ fifteen items on the agenda.

2 Look – _____ any butter in the fridge. _____ a lot yesterday. Did you use it all? And _____ any eggs. Let's go shopping.

3 My old school was really small. _____ a lot of classrooms – only seven, one for each year. But now _____ a new school and it's much bigger and better and _____ a great new snack bar, too.

4 _____ a new football stadium in our town and _____ a big football game there last Saturday. _____ a lot of English fans because it was Bayern Muenchen against Manchester United.

2 Daily routines

2a Now you: Order the activities.
Nummerieren Sie die Aktivitäten in der Reihenfolge, in der Sie sie morgens machen.

☐ wake up ☐ get up
☐ have breakfast ☐ make tea / coffee
☐ clean your teeth ☐ leave the house
☐ have a shower ☐ get dressed

2b Now you: Your morning routine
Schreiben Sie Sätze mit den Verben aus Aufgabe 2a.

HELP
Denken Sie daran immer das **Present simple** zu verwenden, wenn Sie über Dinge sprechen, die Sie **regelmäßig** machen.
Die *He- / She- / It*-Formen der Verben enden immer mit einem *-s*.

2c Write sentences about Sarah's routines.

1 get up – 6 o'clock – every morning
She _____

2 always – drink coffee – in the morning

3 not have breakfast – in the week

4 go to work – twice a week

5 usually – leave the house – 7.30 am

6 never – have a winter holiday

16 sixteen   p. 52

Vocabulary from Unit 2

1 Adjectives

1a A crossword
Lösen Sie das Kreuzworträtsel mit den passenden Adjektiven.

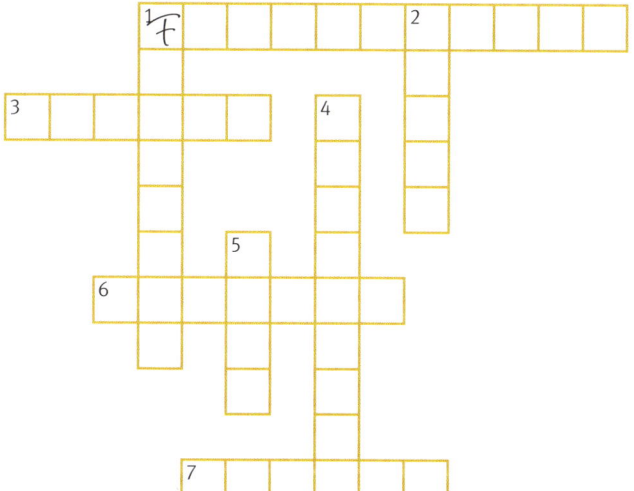

Across:
1. I was interested in the old family photos. They were …
3. The film wasn't interesting, it was …
6. … to meet you.
7. She's lovely – a really … baby.

Down:
1. The hotel receptionist was really helpful and …
2. The weather wasn't good, it was …
4. No, they aren't the same, they're totally …
5. I didn't think the test was difficult, I thought it was …

2 Workplaces

2a Where do they work?

1. h _ _ _ _ l
2. s _ _ p
3. h _ _ _ _ _ _ l
4. o _ _ _ _ e
5. f _ _ _ _ _ y
6. r _ _ _ _ _ _ _ t

2b Now you: Where do you work?

3 Jobs

3a What's his / her job?

1. She works in offices or shops or factories because no-one wants to have a dirty workplace. ____

2. He works in the kitchen of a hotel or a restaurant. ____

3. Some work in hospitals; some have a private practice. ____

4. She works at the front desk of a hotel. She greets people and gives them information. ____

5. This person can work in a factory or in people's homes. You phone him when you have problems with your cooker or your lights. ____

6. This person doesn't have a job now. She worked for many years – but now she's 65 and can relax because she is _ _ _ _ _ _ _ _ _ _ !

Phrases to learn: Talking about your work

I work for (Siemens / my father / a chemicals company).	Ich arbeite für (Siemens / meinen Vater / ein Chemieunternehmen).
I'm (an engineer / a nurse / a housewife).	Ich bin (Ingenieur, Krankenschwester, Hausfrau).
I work in (a bank / a shop / an office).	Ich arbeite in (einer Bank / einem Geschäft / einem Büro).
I work (part time / full time / freelance).	Ich arbeite (teilzeit / vollzeit / freiberuflich).
I'm (retired / unemployed / between jobs).	Ich bin (pensioniert / arbeitslos / zwischen zwei Arbeitsstellen).

 18 **Say it right:** Listen and repeat the sentences.

2 Topic | Ireland

1 **Cities in Ireland** You can see Dublin on the map. Write the names of the other seven towns.

Ireland consists of the Republic of Ireland and Northern Ireland, which is part of the United Kingdom. The Republic of Ireland is a popular tourist destination because of its natural beauty.

Cities in Ireland

Dublin, a city on the east coast, is the capital of Ireland. Its name comes from an old Irish Gaelic phrase *Dubh Linn*, which means *Black Pool*. It has the largest city park in Europe – Phoenix Park; and it has the youngest population of all European cities – about 50% of the people are under 25.

Tullamore is between Dublin and Galway. It's famous for its whiskey – Tullamore Dew. (NB whisk**ey** is Irish; whisk**y** is Scottish.)

Waterford, on the south-east coast, north of Cork, was the starting point of Ryanair. The first flight was a 14-seater plane flying from Waterford to Gatwick.

Sligo, on the north-west coast, looks out onto the Atlantic Ocean. In the Great Famine (1847 – 1851), 30,000 people emigrated to America through the port of Sligo.

Monaghan is just ten kilometres from Northern Ireland. Its name means *Land of the little hills*.

Killarney, in the south-west of Ireland, is the burial place of Rudolf Erich Rasper, the writer of the Münchhausen stories.

Cork, in the south-east, is the second biggest town in the Republic and is the home of a lot of international IT companies. The city has a multi-cutural flair because of the many immigrants from both western and eastern Europe.

Galway, on the west coast, is almost opposite Dublin. This city is the base for Irish television and radio and it's the home of the Irish National Language Theatre.

Most Irish people use English to communicate – but you can see signs in Irish and English.

Glossary: coast – Küste | population – Bevölkerung | flight – Flug | Great Famine – Große Hungersnot | port – Hafen | burial place – Begräbnisstätte

 **Listen to the text.**

2 Guinness

Guinness

The Guinness family is an Anglo-Irish aristocratic family. They made their money in beer-brewing, banking and politics.

Arthur Guinness (1725 – 1803) started brewing dark beer in Dublin in 1759. Six years later, he exported the first Guinness beer – 6 ½ barrels to Great Britain. Today, Guinness makes 850 million litres of beer a year and sells it to 120 different countries.

When you hear the word 'Guinness', maybe you think of beer – or maybe you think of *Guinness World Records*. This is a book which is published every year and contains world records – the biggest pizza, the longest river, the coldest temperature, the most expensive diamond …

The idea for this book came from Sir Hugh Beaver, who was the managing director of Guinness Breweries. In 1951, he had an argument with a friend about the fastest bird in Europe. At that time, there was no reference book to answer that kind of question. So, in 1954, Sir Hugh asked two researchers to compile a book of information about 'the biggest and the best'. In August, 1957, they finished the project – and that Christmas it was the number one best-seller!

And the *Guinness Book of Records* also has a record – it's the book which people most often steal from the library!

🔊 20 **Listen to the text.**

Glossary: beer-brewing – Bierbrauen | barrels – Fässer | sells – verkauft | is published – erscheint | contains – enthält | researchers – Rechercheure, Forscher | steal – stehlen | library – Bücherei

3 Answer the questions.

1 **How** did the Guinness family make their money?

2 **Who** first started the brewing company?

3 **Where** did he start it?

4 **How many** countries can you buy Guinness in?

5 **Which** country was the first to import Guinness?

6 **Whose** idea was it to make a reference book of world records?

7 **What** was his role in the Guinness company?

8 **When** did they publish the first book?

9 **Why** does the *Guinness Book of Records* have a world record?

Four fun facts: Ireland

1 Dublin has 666 pubs and it has the oldest pub in Ireland: *The Brazen Head*. The first record of a pub on this site was in 1198.

2 O'Connell Bridge, over the River Liffey in Dublin, is unique – it's the only bridge in Europe that is as long as it is wide.

3 Bram Stoker, the writer of *Dracula*, was born in Dublin. The title of his famous book comes from two Irish words *Droch Ola* meaning *Bad Blood*.

4 There are no snakes in Ireland.

Glossary: brazen – schamlos, frech | site – Standort | wide – breit | snakes – Schlangen

p. 53

3 Step 1 | Reading

1 Reading: Doc Martens

Doc Martens is the name of a popular kind of shoe. For teenage tourists in London, going to the big Doc Martens shop in Covent Garden is as important as going to Madame Tussauds or the Hard Rock Café. But how 'British' are these shoes? How did it all start?

Klaus Märtens was a doctor in the German army in World War II. In 1945, he was on a skiing holiday in the Bavarian Alps and he fell and injured his foot. His army boots were too uncomfortable, so he made some really comfortable shoes – from tyres!

In 1947, Klaus met an old university friend – Dr Herbert Funck. They went into business together and opened a shoe factory in Seeshaupt. The shoes were a big hit because they were so comfortable. The first people who bought the shoes were housewives – and for the first ten years, 80% of Doc Marten's customers were women over 40!

In 1959, a British shoemaker took over the company. The shoes and boots were popular with factory workers, postmen and police officers – people who were on their feet all day. In the 1970s, skinheads and rock musicians started to wear them. They were the shoes of the British sub-culture – the punks and the skinheads.

Between 1970 and 2010, the company sold over 100 million pairs of shoes! Today the Doc Marten's image is not so wild – even the Pope ordered 100 pairs of the boots for the Swiss Guard – plus one pair of white leather Doc Martens in a size 9 – for himself!

Glossary: injured – verletzte | foot *(plural: feet)* – Fuß | tyres – Reifen | customers – Kunden | took over – übernahm | leather – Leder

> HELP
> **Fragen** im **Past simple** bilden Sie mit *did* (Vergangenheitsform von *do*) oder mit *was / were* (Vergangenheitsformen von *is / are*).

 21 **Listen to the text.**

1a Answer the questions.

1 Where **is** the big Doc Martens shop in London?

2 What **was** Klaus Marten's job in the 1940s?

3 **Did** he injure his knee or his foot?

4 Where **did** Martens and Funck open the first factory?

5 Why **were** the shoes popular with factory workers, postmen and police officers?

6 What **did** the Pope do?

p. 53

Past simple (regular and irregular verbs) 3

2 Grammar

Past simple: Regular verbs

- Mit dem Past simple spricht man über Dinge, die in der Vergangenheit passiert sind.
- Die meisten Verben sind regelmäßge Verben *(regular verbs)*, sie enden mit *-ed*: Martens **injured** his foot.
- Fragen in der Vergangenheit werden mit *Did* und der Grundform des Verbs gebildet: **Did** he **injure** his hand?
- Kurzantwort: **Yes, he did.** / **No, he didn't.**
- Verneinte Sätze werden mit *didn't* und der Grundform des Verbs gebildet: He **didn't injure** his knee.

2a Complete the questions and answers.

1 They opened the first factory in Seeshaupt in 1947.

1a Q: _____ the first factory?
   A: In Seeshaupt.

1b Q: _____ the factory in Austria?
   A: No, it _____, it _____ in Germany.

1c Q: _____ a factory in Augsburg?
   A: No, _____.

1d Q: _____ the Seeshaupt factory?
   A: In 1947.

2 The Pope ordered 100 pairs of black boots for the Swiss Guard.

2a Q: _____ boots or shoes?
   A: _____ shoes, he _____ boots.

2b Q: How _____?
   A: One hundred.

2c Q: _____ all the boots for him?
   A: No, _____.

2d Q: _____ the boots?
   A: Black.

3 Grammar

Past simple: Irregular verbs

- Einige Verben, die man häufig braucht, sind unregelmäßig *(irregular verbs)*:
  He **went** to the Bavarian Alps.
- Fragen und verneinte Sätze mit unregelmäßigen Verben bilden Sie in der gleichen Art wie mit regelmäßigen Verben:
  Did he **go** to Vienna?
  No, he **didn't go** to Austria.

> **HELP**
> Auf Seite 148 Ihres Kursbuchs finden Sie eine Liste einiger **unregelmäßiger Verben**.

3a Irregular verbs in the text on page 20
Which verbs do they come from?

1 fall   fell   4 _____ bought
2 _____ made   5 _____ took
3 _____ met   6 _____ sold

3b Cross out the wrong words.

1 Did you **have** | **had** a pair of Doc Marten's boots when you **was** | **were** a teenager?
2 I didn't **have** | **had** a pair of boots, but I **have** | **had** a pair of Doc's shoes.
3 Where did you **buy** | **bought** them?
4 I **buy** | **bought** them in Covent Garden when I **was** | **were** in London.
5 They **was** | **were** really comfortable.

3 Step 2 | The weather; Compliments; Words easily confused

1 The weather

1a What's the weather like?

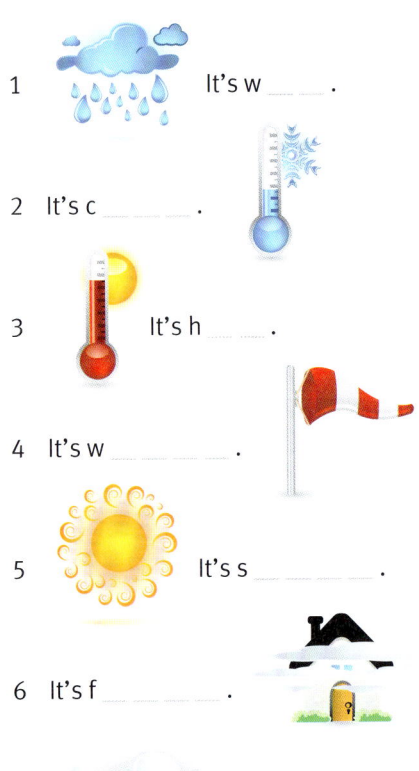

1 It's w_____.
2 It's c_____.
3 It's h_____.
4 It's w_____.
5 It's s_____.
6 It's f_____.
7 It's c_____.

1b Make questions. Ordnen Sie die Wörter, sodass sie eine Frage ergeben.

1 like | What's | in your country? | the weather

2 nice | the weather | Was | yesterday?

3 Which | favourite | is | your | season?

🔘 22 **Say it right:** Listen and repeat the questions.

1c Now you: Answer the questions in exercise 1b.

1 _____
2 _____
3 _____

2 Compliments

2a Complete these compliments.

1 W_____ a lovely day!
2 T_____ is a lovely snack.
3 This curry l_____ good, s_____ great and t_____ wonderful!
4 Your holiday s_____ fantastic!

🔘 23 **Say it right:** Listen and repeat the sentences.

2b Write compliments.

1 _____

2 _____

3 _____

4 _____

3 Words easily confused

3a Cross out the wrong words.

1 I lived in Manchester **as** | **when** I was a child.
2 Thanks very much. – **Please.** | **You're welcome.**
3 **Where** | **Who** do you live?
4 Did you **do** | **make** English at school?
5 I started school **for thirty years** | **thirty years ago.**

Past time phrases; Holidays 3

4 Grammar

Past time phrases

When did you **last** go there?

I went there **yesterday**.
I went there **last week**.
I went there **on Monday**.
I went there **on May 2nd**.
I went there **in 2013**.
I went there **two months ago**.
I went there **when I was 17**.

4a Write the past tense of these verbs.

1	buy	
2	come	
3	drink	
4	eat	
5	get	
6	go	
7	have	
8	see	
9	wear	
10	write	

🔊 24 **Say it right:** Listen and repeat the words.

4b Now you: Complete the sentences.

Ergänzen Sie mindestens fünf der Sätze über sich mit einer Zeitangabe.

1 I was born _____.
2 I started school _____.
3 I started work _____.
4 I got married _____.
5 I had a baby _____.
6 I moved to a new town _____.
7 I started learning English _____.
8 I last went on holiday _____.

5 Holidays

5a Now you: Your last holiday

Beantworten Sie die Fragen und schreiben Sie eine Geschichte über Ihren letzten Urlaub.

When was your last holiday?

Where did you go?

Who did you go with?

How did you travel?

Where did you stay?

How long did you stay?

What was the weather like?

What did you eat and drink?

What were the people like?

What was the best thing?

p. 53

twenty-three 23

3 Step 3 | Invitations; Special events

1 Invitations

1a Complete the invitations.

1 _____ you like to go to the cinema with me?
2 _____ like to go for a drink with me?
3 _____ to go for a meal with me?
4 _____ go to a café with me?
5 _____ to the concert with me?
6 _____ the theatre with me?

 25 **Say it right:** Listen and repeat the questions.

> **HELP**
> When German speakers use the word '**invite**' (= ein-laden), they mean they are going to pay for the treat (= Bewirtung, Vergnügen). In English, '**invite**' means: *I'd like you to come with me.* If you want to pay, tell your guest: *It's my treat.*

1b Complete the replies to the invitations.

1 Thank you, I'd ____o____ to.
2 W_____ a good idea!
3 Yes – what ___b_____ Friday?
4 I'm ___rr___, I can't.

26 **Say it right:** Listen and repeat the sentences.

2 Special events

2a Greeting cards Ordnen Sie die Texte auf den Grußkarten den Situationen zu.

1 He got married and the card said: ☐
2 He was ill and the card said: ☐
3 It was February 14th and the card said: ☐
4 He had a driving test and the card said: ☐
5 It was December 25th and the card said: ☐

a) Happy Christmas
b) Congratulations on your wedding day
c) To my Valentine
d) Get well soon
e) Good luck – hope you pass!

2b Milestones Meilensteine – wählen Sie für jeden Satz das richtige Verb und setzen Sie es im *Past tense* ein.

buy | come | die | kill | land | make | take | win | write

1 Lee Harvey Oswald _____ President Kennedy in 1963.
2 The Berlin Wall _____ down in 1989.
3 Apollo _____ on the moon in 1969.
4 The World Cup _____ place in Germany in 2006.
5 Willy Brandt _____ the Nobel Peace Prize in 1971.
6 J.K. Rowling _____ the Harry Potter books in the 1990s.
7 The US _____ Alaska from Russia in 1867.
8 Apple _____ its first iPhone in 2007.
9 Queen Victoria _____ in 1901.

 27 **Say it right:** Listen and repeat the sentences.

2c Now you: Your milestones
Schreiben Sie fünf Meilensteine aus Ihrem Leben auf.

Vocabulary from Unit 3

1 Numbers, dates and years

1a Write the numbers in words.

a) 2
b) 12
c) 15
d) 98
e) 100

1b Write the dates in words.

a) 31st
b) 22nd
c) 3rd
d) 30th

> **HELP**
> 1903 = Nineteen oh three
> 1956 = Nineteen ~~hundred~~ fifty-six
> 2015 = Twenty fifteen

1c Complete the sentences in words.
(Exercise 2b on page 24 can help you!)

1 Queen Victoria died in

2 J.K. Rowling wrote the Harry Potter books in the

3 Apollo landed on the moon in

4 This year is

2 Clothes

2a Pack her case. Schreiben Sie die Kleidungsstücke, die nur für Frauen sind, in den Koffer.

bikini
blouse
boots
dress
jacket
jeans
pullover
shirt
shoes
shorts
skirt
socks
suit
trousers

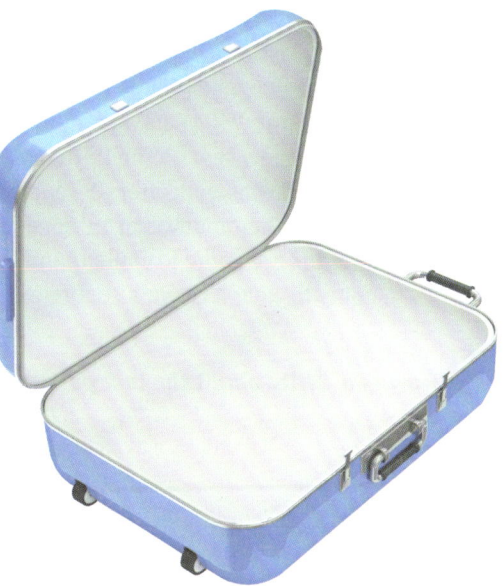

> **HELP**
> *Shorts*, *jeans*, *trousers* sind **Pluralwörter**: *My trousers **are** dirty.*

2b Now you: Your favourite clothes

1 What is your favourite item of clothing?

2 Where did you buy it / them?

3 What colour is it / are they?

4 When did you buy it / them?

5 When did you last wear it / them?

Phrases to learn: Shopping for clothes

Excuse me! Where can I try it on?   *Entschuldigung, wo kann ich es anprobieren?*
It doesn't fit.   *Es passt nicht.*
Have you got it in a different colour, please?   *Haben Sie es bitte in einer anderen Farbe?*
Have you got a size bigger / smaller, please?   *Haben Sie bitte eine Nummer größer / kleiner?*

 28 **Say it right:** Listen and repeat the sentences.

p. 53

3 Topic | A get-together

1 What kind of party is it? Match the right party to 1–8.

a) a wedding reception
b) a house-warming party
c) a golden anniversary party
d) a retirement party
e) a fancy-dress party
f) a New Year's Eve party
g) a dinner party
h) a birthday party

1 ☐ He's 21 today.
2 ☐ We want to welcome friends to our new house.
3 ☐ They got married 50 years ago today.
4 ☐ We do this every year on the thirty-first of December.
5 ☐ It's his last day at work after 45 years!
6 ☐ The marriage ceremony is at 11 am and the party is from 2 pm.
7 ☐ Four friends are going to come round for a meal at 8 pm.
8 ☐ I'm going to wear a clown's costume.

1a Now you: Write about the last party you went to.

_____
_____
_____
_____

2 Conversation starters Lernen Sie diese Ausdrücke, damit Sie nicht in Verlegenheit geraten, wenn Sie Leute auf Parties treffen, die Sie noch nicht kennen.

Where did you meet (name of host)?

Do you know many people here?

Can I get you another drink?

Do you like this music?

3 A note of thanks Nach einer Party ist es höflich sich bei den Gastgebern telefonisch, mit einer Karte oder mit einer E-Mail zu bedanken. Ergänzen Sie diese Danksagung.

_____ Marie and Frank
_____ you for a really _____
party last Saturday. I had a _____ time.
And the food was _____ !
I hope you enjoyed your _____ party, too!
Best wishes,

4 Don't put your foot in it! Treten Sie nicht ins Fettnäpfchen! Lesen Sie über kulturelle Unterschiede und ergänzen Sie das jeweilige Land.

Britain | Germany | India | Japan | the United States

Don't put your foot in it!

1 In _____, it's polite to be punctual or a bit early for business meetings, but don't arrive at someone's house for a social gathering earlier than the time on the invitation. Invitations often say: *Seven-thirty for eight* – this means you can arrive after 7.30 and dinner will be at 8, so it's best to arrive at about 7.45.

2 Offer to take off your shoes when you go into someone's home. And never point your feet at another person because in _____, they think that feet are unclean.

3 At a British party, if you need the toilet, you can say, "*Where's the loo?*". But in _____, they don't like the word *toilet* or *loo*, so they ask, "*Where's the bathroom?*".

4 In _____, you can take a gift for your host – but don't give white flowers or any gift connected with the numbers four or nine because they are unlucky. The gift must be wrapped and given to the host in private – and with both hands. The host opens the gift in private, too.

5 In _____, you can give flowers to your host but not red roses. Give an uneven number of flowers – and you must take the paper off the flowers before you give them.

Glossary: polite – höflich | punctual – pünktlich | point at – richten auf | feet – Füße | loo – Toilette | gift – Geschenk | wrapped – eingepackt | uneven – ungerade

29 **Listen to the texts.**

Four fun facts: Social events

Some social events are very strange – you must see them to believe them!

So type these events into your search engine and watch the people in action!

① Every year in Gloucester, England, where they make the famous cheese, thousands of people come to the **cheese-rolling event**. They roll a big, round cheese down a hill and people run after it. The cheese sometimes travels at 112 kilometres per hour!

② On March 22nd, 2008, the world's biggest pillow fight took place in 25 cities across the world, including Boston, Copenhagen, Dubai, London, Shanghai and Sydney – in New York, 5,000 people took part in the **Worldwide Pillow Fight Day**.

③ On the last Wednesday of August, thousands of tourists come to the town of Bunol in Spain to have a tomato fight! **La Tomatina** festival lasts for one week – but the tomato fight lasts just one hour. People throw one hundred tons of tomatoes at each other – it's like having a bath in spaghetti sauce!

④ Finland, the home of Nokia, the huge telecommunications company, started a new social event in the year 2000: **mobile phone throwing** (AE: cell phone throwing). And now these contests are held every year in lots of countries around the world.

Glossary: strange – seltsam | pillow fight – Kissenschlacht | lasts – dauert | throw at each other – sich gegenseitig bewerfen

p. 53

4 Step 1 | Saying where things are

1 Saying where things are

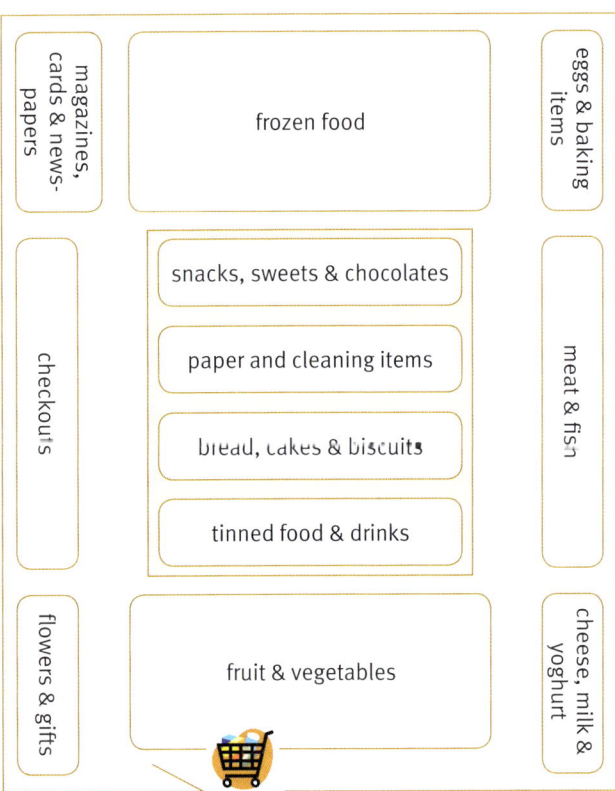

BUYWELL SUPERMARKET

HELP

It's opposite ~~of~~ the checkouts.

1b Where is it?
Look at the places you went to in exercise 1a. Use these words to say where each section is.

in | next to | opposite | near | (2x) between | (3x) on

1 It's _____ the meat and fish counter.
2 It's _____ the left of the frozen food.
3 It's _____ the tinned food.
4 It's _____ the flowers and the cheese sections.
5 It's _____ the fruit and vegetables.
6 It's _____ the middle of the store, _____ the right.
7 They're _____ the left, _____ the gifts and the cards.

1a Where do you go? Schauen Sie sich den Supermarkt-Plan an und schreiben Sie die Abteilungen auf, in die Sie gehen müssen.

1 You want to make a cake and you need flour and sugar.
_____
2 You want to buy *The Times*.
_____
3 You need a little birthday present for your neighbour.
_____
4 You don't have any potatoes.
_____
5 You want four bottles of mineral water.
_____
6 You need some beef for tonight's dinner.
_____
7 And now you have to pay.
_____

HELP

Saying thank you – Um sich bei jemandem zu bedanken, können Sie *Thanks very much* oder *Thanks a lot* sagen. Die Antwort darauf lautet: *You're welcome* oder *It's OK*.

1c Asking where something is
Write in the missing words.

A: (1) E_____ me.
B: Yes?
A: Is (2) t_____ a cash machine (3) n_____ here?
B: Yes, there (4) _____. There's a cash machine (5) i_____ Bridge Street.
A: And where is it (6) e_____?
B: It's inside the post (7) o_____. Look – you can see the church from here and it's (8) n_____ to the church.
A: Oh, right. Thanks very (9) m_____.
B: You're (10) w_____.

28 twenty-eight   p. 53

a / an, *some*, *any*; Places in town; Everyday phrases

4

2 Grammar

a / an, some, any

- *a* steht vor Substantiven, deren erster Laut ein Konsonant *(b, n, r, …)* ist:
  *I need **a** bottle of olive oil.*
- *an* steht vor Substantiven, deren erster Laut ein Vokal *(a, e, i, o, u)* ist:
  *I don't want **an** expensive one.*
- *some* steht in positiven Aussagesätzen:
  *I must buy **some** cheese.*
- *any* steht in verneinten Sätzen und Fragen:
  *I don't need **any** eggs. Do you need **any** eggs?*

HELP

Der **Anfangslaut**, nicht der Anfangsbuchstabe eines Substantivs entscheidet, ob davor *a* oder *an* steht. Wenn Sie z. B. das Wort *hour* [ˈaʊə] aussprechen, hören Sie kein *h* am Anfang – also heißt es *an hour*. Und vor Substantiven, die mit *uni-* [ˌjuːnɪ-] beginnen, steht *a* – z. B. *a university*.

2a Write *a* or *an* before the words.

1 _____ book
2 _____ orange book
3 _____ interesting book
4 _____ new book
5 _____ old book
6 _____ uniform
7 _____ school uniform
8 _____ Italian uniform
9 _____ hour
10 _____ minute

🔊 30 **Say it right:** Listen and repeat.

2b Cross out the wrong words.

1 Do you have **a** | **any** full bottle of wine in your fridge?
2 There isn't **a** | **any** red wine.
3 I have **any** | **some** white wine.
4 I must buy **a** | **some** wine and **a** | **some** olives.
5 I didn't buy **any** | **some** olives at the market.
6 But I bought **any** | **some** nice cheese.
7 And I must buy **a** | **an** pineapple, too.

2c Now you: Your fridge

Was ist in Ihrem Kühlschrank?

In my fridge, …
1 there's a _____
2 there are some _____
3 there aren't any _____

3 Places in town

3a A word puzzle Markieren Sie zwölf Dinge, die Sie in einer Stadt finden können.

S	P	O	S	Y	S	C	P	O	N
C	C	H	U	R	C	H	O	F	O
H	U	X	P	E	H	R	S	F	R
C	A	F	E	F	O	I	T	I	E
M	O	P	R	I	O	L	O	C	S
R	Y	U	M	P	L	Z	F	E	T
T	J	B	A	N	K	I	F	B	A
L	I	B	R	A	R	Y	I	L	U
C	C	K	K	W	U	T	C	O	R
Q	U	E	E	B	H	Z	E	C	A
A	H	O	T	E	L	O	I	K	N
E	V	O	S	R	J	O	P	S	T

3b Use the words to complete the sentences.

Ergänzen Sie die Sätze mit Wörtern aus 3a.

1 You can get something to eat and drink in
  a _____, a _____ and in some _____.
2 There is often a cash machine in a _____ or a _____.
3 _____ are normally the highest buildings in the town.
4 Big _____ are often open 24 hours a day.
5 The _____ is often next to the _____, so that the children can use the books easily.
6 There's a baby polar bear in this _____.

4 Everyday phrases

4a Match the English to the German.

1 It doesn't matter.   5 What a pity!
2 Is it OK if I do that?   6 Be careful!
3 Have a good time.   7 Cheers!
4 See you later.   8 Yes, of course – no problem.

☐ a) Schade!   ☐ e) Viel Spaß.
☐ b) Das macht nichts. ☐ f) Prosit!
☐ c) Ja, natürlich –   ☐ g) Bis später.
     kein Problem.   ☐ h) Ist es in Ordnung, wenn
☐ d) Vorsicht!   ich das mache?

🔊 31 **Say it right:** Listen and repeat the sentences.

4 Step 2 | Shopping; Prices

1 Shopping

1a Complete the phrases.

1 E_____ me.
2 C____ I have a kilo of oranges, please?
3 C_____ I have a pineapple, please?
4 I'd l____ some tomatoes, please.
5 How m_____ are they?
6 Would you like anything _____?
7 That's a ____, thank you.

🔊 32 **Say it right:** Listen and repeat the sentences.

1b Match the halves of the sentences.

1 Could I have a
2 I'd like
3 And I need some
4 I don't need
5 I have a lot of cheese so
6 Do you have

　a) oranges, too.
　b) any aubergines?
　c) bottle of Cola, please?
　d) many eggs – six is fine.
　e) I don't need any today.
　f) a kilo of apples.

🔊 33 **Say it right:** Listen and repeat the sentences.

> **HELP**
> Denken Sie an das Wörtchen *of*, wenn Sie Mengenangaben machen: *A kilo of sugar, a packet of cigarettes, ...*

1c What do you say?

1 You want to know the price of potatoes.
　_____
2 Ask for 5 kg of potatoes.
　_____
3 Say you have all the things you need.
　_____

1d Now you: Your shopping list

Write your grocery and greengrocery shopping list in English. Use a dictionary for words you don't know.

2 Prices

> **HELP**
> 99p = ninety-nine p / ninety-nine pence
> £6.99 = six pounds ninety nine / six ninety-nine

2a Complete the phrases.

1 How *u*____ is it?
2 How much ____ *e* they?
3 How much do they _____ *t*?
4 One costs £6 – that is, £6 *e*_____.
5 You can say 99p or 99 _____ *e*.
6 That's eight *p*_____ forty-nine altogether, please.

🔊 34 **Say it right:** Listen and repeat the sentences.

> **HELP**
> Beachten Sie die **Schreibweise**:
> *eight, twelve, forty, ninety*

2b Write the prices in words.

1 12p _____
2 £8 _____
3 £40.92 _____
4 £52 _____

p. 54

much, many and a lot of; A shopping puzzle

3 Grammar

much, many and *a lot of*

– Zählbare Substantive, z. B. *books, bottles*:
How **many** books do you have? – Not **many**.
I don't have **many** books.
I have **a lot of** magazines.

Wie viele? = How **many**?

– Nicht-zählbare Substantive, z. B. *sugar, wine*:
How **much** wine do you have? – Not **much**.
I don't have **much** wine.
I have **a lot of** beer.

Wie viel? = How **much**?

3a Cross out the wrong words.

1 You can use *much* with **countable | uncountable** nouns.
2 You can use *many* with **countable | uncountable** nouns.
3 You **can | can't** use *a lot of* with both.

HELP

Sie können *euros* und *pounds* zählen, aber nicht *money*: How **many** euros / pounds …? How **much** money …?

Sie können *minutes* und *hours* zählen, aber nicht *time*: How **many** minutes / hours …? How **much** time …?

3b Write in *much* or *many*.

1 How _____ eggs are there in your fridge?
2 How _____ English do you speak outside the classroom?
3 How _____ chocolate do you eat?
4 How _____ free time do you have?
5 How _____ children do you have?

🔊 35 **Say it right:** Listen and repeat the questions.

3c Now you: Answer the questions in exercise 3b.

Not many | Not much | None | A lot

1 _____   4 _____
2 _____   5 _____
3 _____

HELP

When you go shopping in an English supermarket, you sometimes see **BOGOF** on a display of items. BOGOF? = Buy One, Get One Free!

4 A shopping puzzle

Peter, James, Paul and Toby sind im Supermarkt. Lesen Sie die Informationen über diese vier Personen und ordnen Sie ihnen die passenden Einkaufskörbe zu. Streichen Sie die falschen Namen durch.

A
Basket A belongs to
Peter | James | Paul | Toby.

B
Basket B belongs to
Peter | James | Paul | Toby.

C
Basket C belongs to
Peter | James | Paul | Toby.

D
Basket D belongs to
Peter | James | Paul | Toby.

– James is vegetarian and he never buys meat.
– Paul doesn't have many tomatoes in his basket.
– Peter is lactose intolerant – no milk products for him!
– Toby never drinks alcohol.
– There are some eggs in Toby's basket.
– James hates aubergines and pineapples (= *Ananas*).
– Paul has some lemons for his gin and tonics!
– Peter doesn't like broccoli.
– There's a bottle of milk in Paul's basket.

p. 54

4 Step 3 — can / can't, have to / don't have to; What does it stand for?; Reading

1 Grammar

can / can't, have to / don't have to

You **can** use your mobile phone at the airport but you **can't** use it on the plane.

You **have to** go through the security gate but you **don't have to** take off your shoes.

1a What do these airport signs mean?
Complete the sentences.

You have to | You can | You don't have to | You can't

1  _____ go up to the next level.

2  _____ pay to use the Internet.

3  _____ get information here.

4  _____ show your tickets.

5  _____ take drinks through security.

6  _____ turn off your phone.

7 _____ sit down and wait for your plane.

2 What does it stand for?

2a Write in words what these mean.

1 GB = _____
2 UK = _____
3 USA = _____
4 EU = *European Union*
5 £ = _____
6 $ = _____

3 Reading: Duty free shopping

When you are at the airport, you can shop in the duty free shops and buy tax-free items – cigarettes, tobacco, fashion items, perfume, cosmetics, jewellery, electrical items, chocolates, gifts and alcoholic drinks.

When you travel from the EU (European Union) to the UK, you can take an unlimited number of items into the country, but you can't sell them in the UK – the items have to be for your personal use only.

When you travel into the UK from outside the EU, there are restrictions on the number of duty-free items you can take into the UK.

Glossary: tax-free – steuerfrei | unlimited number – unbegrenzte Anzahl | personal use – persönlicher Gebrauch | restrictions – Beschränkungen

🔊 36 **Listen to the text.**

3a True or false?

T F

1 You don't have to pay tax on duty-free items. ☐ ☐
2 You can buy tobacco in the duty free shop. ☐ ☐
3 When you travel to the UK from the EU, there are restrictions on the number of items you can take into the country. ☐ ☐
4 You can sell the duty-free items in the UK. ☐ ☐
5 You can't take any duty-free items into the UK from the USA. ☐ ☐
6 You can take a limited number of duty-free items into the UK from Canada. ☐ ☐

3b Now you: A typical gift
What's a typical gift from your country?

Vocabulary from Unit 4

1 Presents and gifts

1a Put the gifts into the right category.

CHOCOLATESHATCHAMPAGNEBOOK
PHOTOALBUMWINETEAPOTBISCUITS
GAMEMAGAZINEPULLOVERFLOWERS
TEDDYBEARCOFFEEPOT

Two things to read:
Two things to eat:
Two things to drink:
Two things to wear:
Two things to play with:
Two things to use in the kitchen:
Two things to look at:

1b Now you: Gifts and presents

1 What was the last gift that you bought?

2 What was your best birthday present?

3 What gifts do you take to friends' dinner parties?

4 Who is the most difficult person that you have to buy a gift for? Why?

2 Food and drink

2a Write the words. Ordnen Sie die Buchstaben und schreiben Sie die Nahrungsmittel bzw. Getränke auf.

1 seeech
2 toopates
3 sgeg
4 dearb
5 atem
6 oonnis
7 cocohatle
8 hourgty
9 graneos
10 cfefeo
11 ate
12 lisaam
13 ttbreu
14 pous

3 Shopping quantities

3a Complete the words.

1 a b_____ of shampoo
2 a p_____ of biscuits
3 a k_____ of tomatoes
4 a b____ of potatoes
5 a j____ of jam
6 a t____ of soup
7 a p_____ of cheese

37 **Say it right:** Listen and repeat.

Phrases to learn: Shopping

Could I have a kilo of tomatoes, please?	Könnte ich bitte 1 Kilo Tomaten bekommen?
How much are they?	Wie viel kosten sie?
I'd like a pineapple, please.	Ich hätte gern eine Ananas, bitte.
How much is it?	Wie viel kostet sie?
And I need some apples.	Und ich brauche ein paar Äpfel.
That's all, thank you.	Das ist alles, danke.

38 **Say it right:** Listen and repeat the sentences.

4 Topic | Shopping

1 **Supermarket tricks**

Supermarket tricks

Do you buy more than you need when you go shopping in supermarkets?
A lot of supermarkets use marketing strategies to make their customers buy more items than they really need.

First, when you go into the store, you can hear relaxing music so that you feel you don't have to hurry. *(Slow music makes you shop for longer and buy 29 % more; classical music makes you buy more expensive items.)* There are only six items on your shopping list so you don't really need a big shopping cart – but there are no baskets. *(When supermarkets use big carts, shoppers buy 19 % more.)*

The first section is fruit and vegetables – they look really fresh and appetising *(someone sprays them with water twice a day)* so you buy some strawberries. And some asparagus – that's on your list. Ah – there are packets of Hollandaise sauce next to the asparagus – that's practical. *(Placing items that complement each other means a shopper buys two items, not just one.)* Mmmm. There's a fantastic smell of bread – maybe you should buy a baguette for supper? Or some of those nice little cakes? *(Supermarkets are designed so that you have to walk past the bakery and / or the cooked meats section and the appetising smell tempts shoppers to buy things spontaneously.)* You need some milk – but that's at the opposite end of the store. *(So you have to walk through the store and you see more products.)* Look! Is that a special offer on biscuits? *(95 % of shoppers only know the price of milk, bread, bananas and eggs – they have little idea of other prices.)* There's a big red sign *(red is associated with special offers)*: Giant packets (500g) £4.50. Sounds good – and the children love those. *(Look at the price of a 250g packet – £2.20.)* Now you're at the shelves of pasta and, of course, you compare the prices. *(But don't only compare the packets at eye-level, look on the lower shelves, too – that's where supermarkets often put their own, cheaper, brands.)*

Go to the checkout. There are six people in front of you so you look around – and see chocolate bars. Yes, you are a bit hungry so maybe you should buy a few of those. *(Snack items are near the checkout – shoppers want a reward.)* Oh dear, there are lots of things in the cart, not only the six things on your shopping list. Maybe take something out of the cart – but where to put it? *(Checkouts are designed so it's difficult for shoppers to leave an item.)* Oh well, find your loyalty card … if you spend more than £50, you get a 5 % discount!

Glossary: store – Geschäft | hurry – sich beeilen | shopping cart – Einkaufswagen | asparagus – Spargel | practical – praktisch | smell – Duft | supper – Abendessen | tempts – verleitet | special offer – Sonderangebot | shelf *(pl. shelves)* – Regal | compare – vergleichen | eye-level – Augenhöhe | lower – niedrigeren | chocolate bars – Schokoriegel | reward – Belohnung | leave – zurücklassen | loyalty card – Kundenkarte

39 **Listen to the text.**

> **HELP**
> Gibt es ein paar **unbekannte Wörter** im Text? Keine Sorge, auch wenn Sie nicht jedes Wort in einem Text verstehen, werden Sie die wesentlichen Informationen erfassen.

2 **Answer the questions.**

1 What happens if the supermarket has classical music in the background?

2 Why do you think a lot of supermarkets don't have baskets?

3 What smells tempt shoppers?

4 It's important where items are displayed in the supermarket. Underline four examples of this in the text.

 p. 54

3 Now you: What kind of shopper are you?

What role does shopping play in your life? Are you a shopaholic or a shopaphobic?
Try this personality test and find out.

What kind of shopper are you?

1 How many times a week do you go shopping for food?
- a) Every day.
- b) Once or twice a week.
- c) Only when you need something.

2 When you go food shopping, do you …
- a) have no plan – just buy spontaneously?
- b) buy what you need, but buy other things, too?
- c) only buy what's on your shopping list?

3 When you go on holiday, do you …
- a) plan shopping trips to different places?
- b) enjoy buying local products from local markets?
- c) stay away from the shops?

4 When you buy clothes, do you …
- a) try on several items in different shops before you decide?
- b) go to your favourite shop and try on one or two items?
- c) buy what you think is OK and try it on at home?

5 When you go clothes shopping, you think:
- a) I have my credit card with me so I don't have to worry how much I spend.
- b) I can pay by card – but I must be careful how much I spend.
- c) I know how much money I have with me and I can't spend more than that.

6 How much time do you normally spend in a clothes store?
- a) Over an hour.
- b) 10-15 minutes.
- c) In and out.

7 When you see the sign *75% discount*, do you …
- a) buy something even if it isn't exactly what you want?
- b) look at the items for a few minutes to see if there is anything for you?
- c) walk away from the chaos?

For each a) answer, you get 3 points. For each b) answer, you get 2 points. For each c) answer, you get 1 point.

Your total: ☐

Now look at page 54 to find out what kind of shopper you are.

Four fun facts: Online shopping

1 In January 2006, a British man sold a brussel sprout (cooked on Christmas Day and frozen) on eBay for £1550 ($2100.72 USD). The money went to cancer research.

2 Also in that year, an Australian tried to sell New Zealand on eBay. The starting price was one cent. After 22 bids, the price reached $3000 – but then eBay took New Zealand off their auction list.

3 In 2008, a python ate four golf balls (he thought they were chicken's eggs!). A vet removed them from the snake's stomach and the balls were auctioned on eBay for $1,400. (The snake recovered.)

4 The window used by Lee Harvey Oswald when he shot President John F. Kennedy was sold on eBay for over 3 million dollars!

Glossary: brussel sprout – Rosenkohl | frozen – eingefroren | cancer research – Krebsforschung | bids – Gebote | reached – erreichte | auction – Auktion | vet – Tierarzt | removed – entfernte | stomach – Magen | recovered – erholte sich, wurde wieder gesund | shot – erschoss

You can find more crazy auctions by typing *strange buys on ebay* into your search engine.

5 Step 1 | Phoning; Travel

1 Phoning

1a Write the phrases in the right box.
Diese Ausdrücke können Sie beim Telefonieren nutzen – einige am Beginn, andere am Ende eines Telefonats. Schreiben Sie sie in das richtige Kästchen.

Bye – see you next week. | This is (Liz). | Is that (Sam)? | Thanks for phoning. | I'd like to ask about ... | How are you? | It was nice to talk to you. | I have to go now.

Start of the call

_____
_____
_____
_____

End of the call

_____
_____
_____
_____

HELP

Legen Sie sich eine Liste mit nützlichen Ausdrücken fürs **Telefonieren** auf Ihren Büroschreibtisch. So sind Sie gewappnet, falls Sie einen Anruf aus England erhalten. Sehr hilfreich ist z. B.: *Could you please email me with your enquiries? / the information?*

1b Match the telephone phrases.

1. Can I have some information about ...?
2. Could I speak to ...?
3. I'd like to thank you for ...
4. I'd like to invite you to ...
5. I'd like to ask for your help ...
6. I want to say sorry for ...
7. I just want to chat.

___ a) Ich will nur plaudern.
___ b) Ich will mich für ... entschuldigen.
___ c) Könnte ich mit ... sprechen?
___ d) Ich würde Sie gerne um Ihre Hilfe bitten.
___ e) Kann ich ein paar Informationen über ... bekommen?
___ f) Ich würde Sie gerne zu ... einladen.
___ g) Ich würde mich gerne bei Ihnen für ... bedanken.

1c Complete the phone conversation.

A: Hello, t_____ is Petra.
B: Hi Petra. H_____ are you?
A: Fine, thanks. Bill, c_____ I speak to Sue, please?
B: I'm s_____, she isn't in at the m_____.
A: Don't w_____. I can phone back l_____.

2 Travel

HELP

by plane, by taxi, by bus, by car – **on** *foot*

2a How did they go there?
Verwenden Sie Ausdrücke mit *by ...* und *on ...* wie im HELP-Kästchen oben und ergänzen Sie die Sätze.

1 I flew. = I went _____.
2 I drove. = I went _____.
3 I cycled. = I went _____.
4 I walked. = I went _____.

2b How did they travel?

1 No, I didn't go by bike. It isn't far and the weather was nice – and I enjoyed the exercise.

2 Friday afternoon in the rush hour – I wanted to park and take the bus!

3 Can you take me to the Odeon Cinema, please? Do you know it? It's in Brent Street.

4 I'd like a day-return to Glasgow, please. Which platform does it leave from?

5 Yes, I just have hand-luggage.

6 When it started to rain, I cycled as fast as I could – but I got wet through!

1 _____   4 _____
2 _____   5 _____
3 _____   6 _____

p. 54

5 American English and British English; Comparatives

2c A train ticket
Answer the questions.

[Train ticket: STD STD DAY SINGLE, Adult ONE, Child NIL, SGL. Start date 24·MAY·15. Number 63187 82100663-48. From GATWICK AIRPORT. Valid until 24·MAY·15. Price £8·30 M. To BRIGHTON. Route ANY PERMITTED. 1435. SINGLE. Printed 14:35 on 24·MAY·15]

1 When did he travel?

2 Where did he travel from?

3 Where did he travel to?

4 Was the ticket for a child?

5 How much was the ticket?

6 Was it a single (one way) or a return (round trip) ticket?

7 Was it an American or a British ticket?

3 AE (American English) and BE (British English)

3a Match the British and American words.

1 single ticket   a) highway
2 railway   b) truck
3 car park   c) round trip ticket
4 motorway   d) one-way ticket
5 lorry   e) railroad
6 petrol   f) parking lot
7 underground   g) gas
8 return ticket   h) subway

4 Grammar

Comparatives

Short adjectives:
> Cycling is **faster than** walking.
> My car is **bigger than** yours.

Adjectives with *-y* on the end:
> Cycling is **healthier than** driving.

Long adjectives:
> The train is **more expensive than** the bus.

** There are exceptions to these rules, e. g.:
> This airport is ~~moderner~~ **more modern than** Heathrow.

4a Write the comparative form.

1 slow: *slower than*
2 comfortable:
3 pretty:
4 nice:
5 hot:
6 popular:
7 friendly:
8 beautiful:
9 dirty:
10 old:

4b Write in the correct form of the adjective.

1 King's Cross station is (interesting) _____ because Harry Potter films were made there.

2 Paddington, where the express train to Heathrow leaves from, is (busy) _____ than King's Cross.

3 Victoria is (old) _____ than those two stations – it was built in 1860, but London Bridge station, built in the 1830s, is even _____ .

4 Waterloo is (big) _____ than Victoria – it has 130 ticket gates.

5 St Pancras is known as 'the cathedral of stations' – it's (beautiful) _____ than all other London stations.

p. 54

thirty-seven 37

5 Step 2 | Superlatives; Directions

1 Grammar

Superlatives

Short adjectives:
Cycling is faster than walking – but flying is **the fastest**.
My car is bigger than yours – but my wife's car is **the biggest**.

Adjectives with -y on the end:
Cycling is healthier than driving – but walking is **the healthiest**.

Long adjectives:
The train is more expensive than the bus – but a taxi is **the most expensive**.

** There are exceptions to these rules, e. g.:
This airport is more modern than Heathrow – but Dubai is the ~~modernest~~ **most modern** airport.

1a Cross out the wrong words.

1 Noah is the **most popular** | **more popular** boy's name in the US this year.
2 New York is the **bigger** | **biggest** city in the US – it's much bigger **than** | **then** Washington.
3 Hartsfield-Jackson Atlanta International Airport is the **busiest** | **most busy** airport in the world – it has **more** | **most** passengers than any other airport.

1b Now you: Complete the sentences about you.

1 _____ is my (busy) _____ time of the year.
2 _____ is the (beautiful) _____ city I know.
3 _____ is the (difficult) _____ language to learn.
4 _____ is the (old) _____ person in my family.
5 _____ is the (interesting) _____ place to visit in my town.
6 _____ is the (big) _____ shop in my town.
7 _____ is my (nice) _____ colleague at work.

2 Directions

2a Asking for directions
Complete the phrases.

1 E_____ me, is there a park n_____ here?
2 C_____ you t_____ me the w_____ to the bus stop, please?
3 W_____' the n_____ petrol station, please?

🔊 40 **Say it right:** Listen and repeat the questions.

2b Use the phrases above to ask the way.

1 You want to get some money from a machine.

2 You want to change some money.

3 You want to do some shopping.

4 You want to watch a film.

5 You want to have an Italian meal.

6 You want to catch a train.

7 You want to buy some shoes.

p. 54 f.

38 thirty-eight

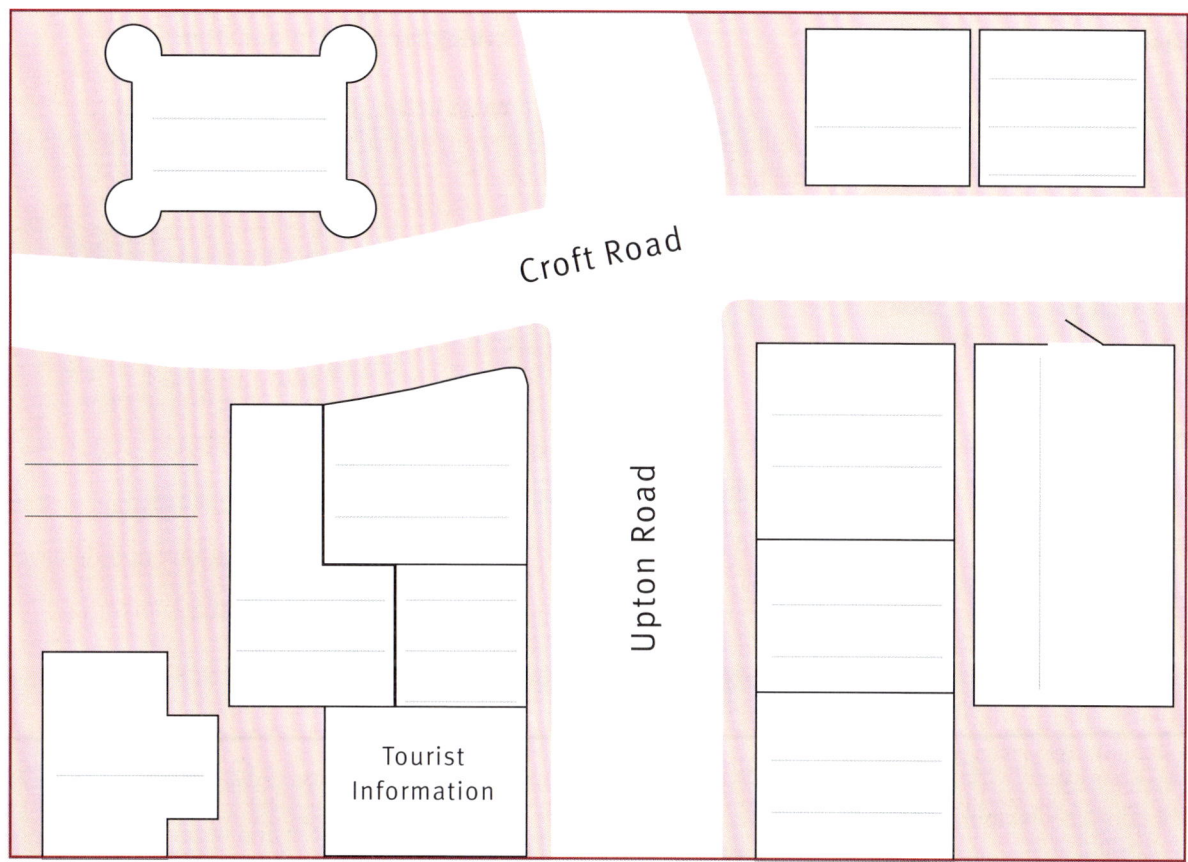

2c **Write these places on the map.**

- The **shoe shop** is opposite the Tourist Information office – just across Upton Road.
- And the Taj Mahal **Indian restaurant** is between the shoe shop and the **post office**.
- There's a new **supermarket** behind that block – the entrance is in Croft Road.
- There's a five-star hotel, **Haddon Hotel,** on the corner of Croft Road and Upton Road – it's directly opposite the post office.
- Some hotel guests have a lovely view of **Haddon Park** and the **church**.
- The hotel shares the **car park** with the **Haddon Arms Pub** next door.
- **Haddon Castle** is in Croft Raod. It's very expensive to go into the castle – maybe that's why there's a **bank** so near – just a bit further along Croft Road!
- And on the right of the bank there's a really good art gallery – **Haddon Art Gallery,** of course.

2d **Follow the directions.** Überprüfen Sie zuerst, ob Sie die Karte in Aufgabe 2c richtig beschriftet haben. – Sie befinden sich vor der *Tourist Information* in der Upton Road. Folgen Sie den Wegbeschreibungen 1–5 und schreiben Sie jeweils auf, wo Sie hinkommen.

1 Go along Upton Road and take the first left. Cross the main road and you'll see it in front of you.

2 Walk down Upton Road and turn right at the crossroads. Now you're in Croft Road. Go past the post office and it's the next building on the right.

3 It isn't far – you can walk from here. Go along this road and it's on the corner at the crossroads – on your left.

4 Go down Upton Road, turn right at the post office, cross over and you're there! It's just after the bank.

5 I think you can see it from here. Look! It's that building next to the shoe shop. You just have to cross the road.

5 Step 3 — *good, better, the best / bad, worse, the worst*; Asking for travel information

1 Grammar

good, better, the best / bad, worse, the worst

I had a **good** holiday but my winter holiday was **better**. My first skiing holiday was **the best** holiday ever!

The hotel I stayed in was really **bad**. The nearby bed and breakfast is **worse**. But **the worst** place to stay is the local pub.

1a Write in *good, better, best, bad, worse* or *worst*.

1. *Titanic* is awful! Before I saw *Titanic*, I thought *Love Story* was the _____ film ever – but *Titanic* is even _____. How can _____ films make so much money?

2. I went to a really _____ Italian restaurant last week – the pizzas were fantastic – even _____ than at *Mario's*. In fact, it's the _____ restaurant I know.

1b Now you: Write about your town.

e.g. attractive: *The Town Hall is the most attractive building.*

1. cheap: _____
2. expensive: _____
3. good: _____
4. new: _____
5. interesting: _____
6. bad: _____
7. big: _____
8. busy: _____

2 Asking for travel information

2a Write in the correct question word.

1. _____ is the last train to Stratford?
2. _____ platform does it leave from?
3. _____ is platform 6?
4. _____ long does it take?
5. _____ time does it arrive?
6. _____ much is a return ticket?

🔊 41 **Say it right:** Listen and repeat the questions.

2b Match the answers to the questions in exercise 2a.

- a) One hour and twenty minutes.
- b) Over there – behind the coffee shop.
- c) The last one leaves at 10.20.
- d) £9.30.
- e) Platform 6.
- f) It gets in at twenty to twelve – if there are no delays.

2c Say it differently.

Replace the phrases in bold with an alternative expression which means the same.

1. Excuse me. **What time** is the next train to Bath?

2. There's a train at **twenty-one thirty**.

3. It **gets in** at midnight.

4. **What does** a single ticket **cost**?

5. Are there any **hold-ups**?

40 forty 🔑 p. 55

Vocabulary from Unit 5 — 5

1 Numbers

1a Look at the picture of a hotel reception.
Beantworten Sie die Fragen in Worten.

1 What time is it?

2 What's the date?

3 How many floors does the hotel have?

4 How much is the cheapest single room?

5 What time is breakfast?

6 What's the woman's room number?

7 What's the latest you can check out?

2 In the street

2a Complete the words.

1 It's dangerous to cross a busy m_____ r_____.

   Look for a z_____ c_____.

2 The bank? Just walk to the c_____

   – you can see the t_____ l_____

   from here. And the bank is on the c_____ of
   King Street and Albert Road.

3 Cross over the railway b_____. Then you can

   see the railway s_____ in front of you.

3 Transport

3a Write the letters in the right box.

a) boarding card b) driver (2x) c) helmet d) petrol (2x)
e) pilot f) rider g) ticket (2x) h) tip i) pump

🚴	✈️
🚌	🚕

Phrases to learn: Travelling

When's the next train to …?	Wann fährt der nächste Zug nach …?
What time does it leave / arrive?	Um wie viel Uhr fährt er ab / kommt er an?
Which platform does it leave from?	Von welchem Gleis fährt er ab?
Do I have to change?	Muss ich umsteigen?
How much is a single / return ticket?	Wie viel kostet eine einfache Fahrkarte/ Rückfahrkarte?

42 **Say it right:** Listen and repeat the questions.   p. 55

5 Topic | Journeys

1 Animals' journeys

The ruby-throated humming bird

Ruby-throated humming birds are very small birds that are only about 8 centimetres long and weigh 3 or 4 grams. Their legs are so short that they have problems walking! These beautiful metallic green and red birds live in Eastern United States and Eastern Canada but, every autumn, they migrate to Mexico. It's an 800-kilometre non-stop flight which takes them about 20 hours – and their tiny wings beat 53 times a second.

Glossary: ruby-throated – Rubinrotkehl… | weigh – wiegen | tiny – winzig | wings – Flügel | beat – schlagen

Ham the astrochimp

Ham the chimpanzee was America's first astronaut. His name was an acronym of Holloman Aerospace Medical center, where he and 40 other chimps did their training. Ham was chosen as the most suitable chimp for the job. In January, 1961, Ham made a suborbital flight which lasted 16 minutes. His spacecraft landed safely in the Atlantic Ocean. Then Ham retired and lived in the National Zoo in Washington until he died in 1983 at the age of 26.

Glossary: was chosen – wurde ausgewählt | suitable – geeignet | suborbital flight – Suborbitalflug | spacecraft – Raumschiff

Sophie Tucker – an Australian cattle dog

In November, 2009, Janet and Dave Griffith took their dog, Sophie Tucker, on a boat trip around the Whitsunday Islands, off the coast of Australia. The waters were rough and the dog fell overboard. Janet and Dave looked for Sophie for over an hour but couldn't find her. They knew there were sharks in that part of the ocean, so they feared the worst. But what they didn't know was that Sophie survived. She swam over 9 kilometres to an uninhabited island and she survived by eating wildlife and drinking river water. Four months later, visiting park rangers found Sophie and they contacted Janet and Dave. All three of them were overjoyed!

Glossary: rough – rauh | sharks – Haie | feared the worst – befürchteten das Schlimmste | survived – überlebte | uninhabited – unbewohnt | rangers – Ranger | overjoyed – außer sich vor Freude

You can see Sophie on Youtube. Type **Sophie Tucker Australian dog** into your search engine.

43 **Listen to the texts.**

2 Write in *The bird*, *Ham* or *Sophie*.

1 _____ made the longest journey.
2 _____ had the closest contact to its owners.
3 _____ 's journey is not unusual for this species.
4 _____ was chosen for the journey.
5 _____ is the most colourful.
6 _____ can swim well.

p. 55

3 Transport quiz

1. Which is the oldest underground train system?
   - a) The Paris Metro
   - b) The New York Subway
   - c) The London Tube

2. Who was the first president of the Ford motor company?
   - a) Gerald Ford
   - b) Harrison Ford
   - c) Henry Ford

3. Where must you drive on the left?
   - a) In Canada
   - b) In Japan
   - c) In Sweden

4. Where is Schipol Airport?
   - a) In Amsterdam
   - b) In Brussels
   - c) In Vienna

5. Which station can you see in the Harry Potter films?
   - a) Victoria
   - b) King's Cross
   - c) Paddington

4 Remember the words.
Schreiben Sie die Wörter auf, die Ihnen im Zusammenhang mit diesen Transportmitteln einfallen.

trains

planes

cars

Four fun facts: The London Tube (The Underground)

1 Over 50% of the network isn't underground, it's above ground.

2 About 3 million people travel on the 400 kilometres of tracks every day.

3 About ½ a million mice live on the London Underground.

4 In 1924, a baby was born on the Underground. Her name? – **T**helma, **U**rsula, **B**eatrice, **E**leanor

Glossary: above ground – oberirdisch | tracks – Schienen | mice – Mäuse

p. 55

forty-three **43**

6 Step 1 | going to – statements

1 Grammar

going to – statements

Going to verwenden Sie, um über Ihre Pläne, d. h. über Dinge, die Sie fest vorhaben, zu sprechen.

I**'m going to** talk about my family and he**'s going to** talk about his native town.
They **aren't going to** talk for more than 30 minutes.

1a What are they going to do?

1 She _____ .

2 They _____ .

3 He _____ .

4 I _____ .

🔊 44 **Say it right:** Listen and repeat the sentences.

1b Negatives
Wandeln Sie die Sätze aus Aufgabe 1a in verneinte Sätze um.

1 _____
2 _____
3 _____
4 _____

HELP

going to + go – Man kann ganz korrekt sagen: *I'm going to go to work tomorrow*, aber das klingt ein bisschen doppelt. Daher sagt man meistens: *I'm going to work tomorrow*.

1c Make sentences with *go*.

1 He – supermarket – later
_____

2 They – Paris – in summer
_____

3 I – work – on Monday
_____

4 The children – school – 8 o'clock
_____

🔊 45 **Say it right:** Listen and repeat the sentences.

1d Where are they going tomorrow?

1 They want to see the new James Bond film.
_____

2 She needs to change euros into dollars.
_____

3 He's got toothache.
_____

4 They've got tickets for a Shakespeare play.
_____

5 Her hair is too long.
_____

6 The children want to see the baby polar bear.
_____

7 She'd like to have an Indian meal tomorrow.
_____

1e Now you: Complete these sentences about you.
Schreiben Sie bejahte oder verneinte Sätze.

1 _____ a cigarette later.

2 _____ TV later.

3 _____ my English homework later.

4 _____ the newspaper later.

5 _____ an email later.

6 _____ a phone call later.

p. 55

Future time phrases; Preparing a presentation   6

1f **Finding information** Schauen Sie sich die beiden Flugtickets an und verwenden Sie *going to*, um so viele Details wie möglich über Silvias und Peters Reise aufzuschreiben.

> **HELP**
> Zwischen Deutschland und England gibt es einen **Zeitunterschied** – die Zeit in England ist 1 Stunde hinter der Zeit in Deutschland.

English Airways

Silvia & Peter May

Flight	BA 763	19 June
Economy class		
From Frankfurt		11.50
To London Gatwick		12.20

English Airways

Silvia & Peter May

Flight	BA 264	27 June
Economy class		
From London Gatwick		07.50
To Frankfurt		10.20

1g **Now you: Write about your holiday plans.**

2 **Future time phrases**

2a **Future time phrases** Unterstreichen Sie die Ausdrücke, die Sie verwenden können, um über die Zukunft zu sprechen.

last week | next week | tomorrow | two weeks ago | when I was a child | in 2025 | the day before yesterday | next year | the day after tomorrow | in two years' time | yesterday | soon

2b **Now you: Complete the sentences about your plans.**
Verwenden Sie *going to*.

1 After the lesson, …

2 Next weekend, …

3 Tomorrow morning, …

4 At Christmas, …

5 When I have time, …

6 On my next summer holiday, …

7 On my next birthday, …

3 **Preparing a presentation**

3a **Match the phrases with a similar meaning.**

1 First, I'd like to introduce myself.
2 I'd like to start by …
3 Next, we're going to look at …
4 To finish off, we're going to …
5 Do you have any questions?

- [ ] a) Are there any questions?
- [ ] b) I'm going to begin by …
- [ ] c) Then we want to look at …
- [ ] d) Finally, we're going to …
- [ ] e) To start off, let me introduce myself.

6 Step 2 | *going to* – questions and short answers; Reading

1 Grammar

going to – questions and short answers

Going to verwenden Sie, um über Ihre Pläne zu sprechen.

Are you going to do the next course?
– Yes, I am. / No, I'm not.

Is she going to teach the A2 course?
– Yes, she is. / No, she isn't.

Are the students going to have a break?
– Yes, they are. / No, they aren't.

1a Write questions with *going to*.

1 they – do – the next course – after the holiday?

2 he – have – a holiday – when the course ends?

3 the English course – continue – next term?

4 you – stop – learning English – when this course ends?

5 she – buy – the A2 coursebook – before the new course starts?

6 we – meet – in the holidays – to practise English?

🎧 46 **Say it right:** Listen and repeat the questions.

1b Match the answers to the questions in exercise 1a.

☐ a) Yes, it is.
☐ b) Yes, they are.
☐ c) Yes, we are.
☐ d) No, I'm not.
☐ e) No, he isn't.
☐ f) Yes, she is.

2 Reading: New Year's resolutions

At the end of December, many of us start to think about New Year's Resolutions.

Typical resolutions?
I'm going to stop smoking.
I'm going to drink less.
I'm going to do more exercise.
I'm going to eat more healthily.
I'm going to spend more time with the family.

Do these sound familiar to you?

But what about making more original resolutions? Here are some ideas:

⇨ Take a selfie in five interesting places.
⇨ Eat a new kind of food every month.
⇨ Turn off your smartphone more often.
⇨ Make a compliment to someone every day.
⇨ Don't spend a whole day in the house.
⇨ Don't spend time with people you don't like – there are 6 billion people in the world!
⇨ Stop throwing away food.
⇨ Listen to different kinds of music.
⇨ Put your unwanted clothes in a collection bin.
⇨ Contact friends and family more often.
⇨ Don't spend so much time online.
⇨ Smile more.
⇨ Learn a good party trick.

Glossary: New Year's resolution – Neujahrsvorsatz | familiar – bekannt, vertraut | selfie – Selfie (digitaler Schnappschuss) | whole – ganzen | throw away – wegwerfen | collection bin – Sammelbehälter | smile – lachen

2a Choose a resolution.

- Highlight the resolutions you'd like to try.
- If you want to try the last one, you can get ideas online:

Type **Video jug** into your search engine. (This is a great site that shows you how to do all kinds of things!) Then search for **Party tricks**. Have fun!

p. 55

6 Your future; Saying goodbye

3 Your future

3a Now you: Write the short answers.

1 Are you going to do the A2 course?

2 Do you want to stay in the same class?

3 Would you like to learn more English?

4 Do you plan to have a break from English?

3b Now you: Complete the sentences about you.
Schreiben Sie Sätze über Ihre zukünftigen Pläne.

1 I might   .

2 I'm going to   .

3 I'd like to   .

4 My plan is to   .

5 I want to   .

6 I'm not going to   .

7 I don't want to   .

4 Saying goodbye

4a Write in the missing words.

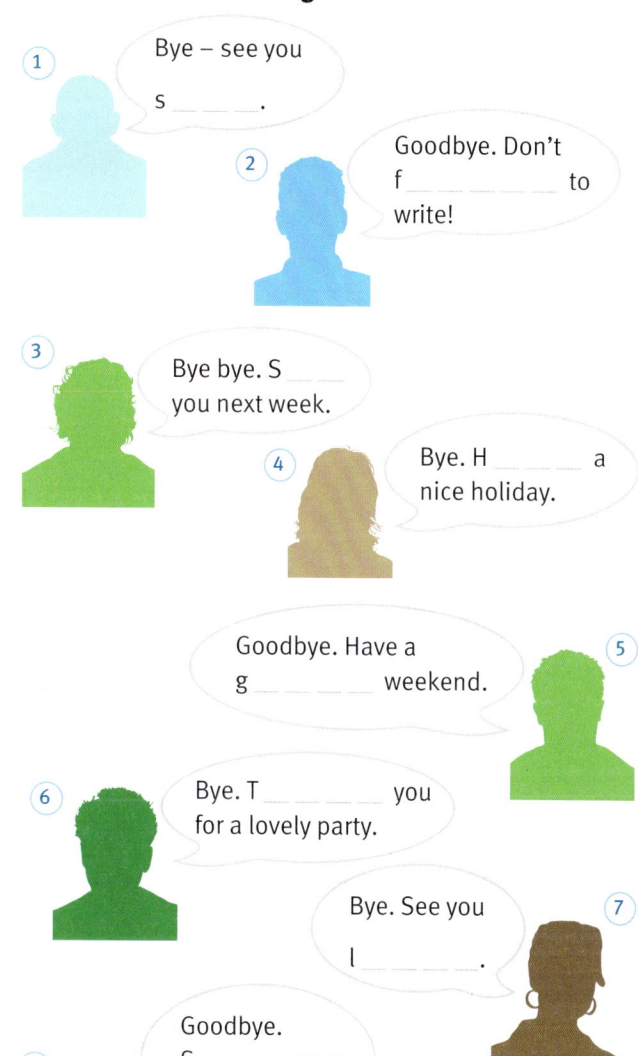

1 Bye – see you s_____.

2 Goodbye. Don't f_____ to write!

3 Bye bye. S_____ you next week.

4 Bye. H_____ a nice holiday.

5 Goodbye. Have a g_____ weekend.

6 Bye. T_____ you for a lovely party.

7 Bye. See you l_____.

8 Goodbye. S_____ us a postcard.

 47 **Say it right:** Listen and repeat the sentences.

4b Goodbye

The word *goodbye* is a short form of *God be with you* (= *Gott sei mit dir*.). In a text from 1659, we can read: *God b'wy*. By 1694, we see *Good-b'wy*. And today, we say: *Goodbye*. Here are some more ways to say *goodbye*:

Cheers!   *Cheerio.*   *So long.* (AE)

Bye for now.   *Take care.*

p. 55

6 Step 3 | Making an appointment; Review of tenses

1 Making an appointment

1a Match the halves of the sentences and write them below.

1 I'd like to make
2 Would Tuesday afternoon
3 I'm sorry,
4 What about
5 Yes, Friday

a) be OK for you?
b) Friday morning?
c) an appointment for a check-up.
d) I can't come on Tuesday.
e) is fine with me.

_____

_____

_____

_____

_____

🔊 48 **Say it right:** Listen and repeat the sentences.

1b Put this conversation in the right order.

R = Receptionist, P = Patient

[1] R: Good morning. Hillside Dental Surgery. Can I help you?
[ ] P: OK. Thanks very much. See you then.
[ ] P: Yes, that's fine.
[ ] P: Do you have anything later – I work till 4.30.
[ ] R: Fine – see you on Friday.
[ ] R: Would Friday morning be OK for you? At 10?
[ ] P: Hello. This is Anne Crowson. I'd like to make an appointment for a check-up, please.
[ ] R: How about 5pm?

1c Now you: When was your last dentist's appointment?

2 Grammar

Review of tenses

Past   I **saw** him last week.
I **didn't see** him yesterday.
When **did** you **see** him?

Present   I **see** him every week.
I **don't see** him at the weekends.
When **do** you **see** him?
She sometimes **sees** him.
She **doesn't see** him very often.
How often **does** she **see** him?

Future   I'**m going to see** him next week.
I'**m not going to see** him tomorrow.
When **are** you **going to see** him?
She'**s going to see** him later.

2a Write the sentences.

Past

 1 the lesson – begin – at 7pm

_____.

2 he – speak – a lot of English

_____?

3 they – not write – a lot of emails

_____.

Present

 1 the lesson – begin – at 7pm

_____.

2 he – speak – a lot of English

_____?

3 they – not write – a lot of emails

_____.

Future

 1 the lesson – begin – at 7pm

_____.

2 he – speak – a lot of English

_____?

 3 they – not write – a lot of emails

_____.

🔑 p. 55 f.

Vocabulary from Unit 6

1 Putting information in order

1a What did she do?

First of all … | Then … | After that … | And finally …

Verwenden Sie diese Satzanfänge, um die Ereignisse in eine chronologische Reihenfolge in der Vergangenheit zu bringen. Beginnen Sie so: *First of all, (she got up) …*

1 get up – have a shower and get dressed – eat breakfast and listen to the news – go to work

2 decide where to go – buy tickets and find her passport – book a hotel – leave for a holiday

1b Now you: Your morning routine

Verwenden Sie die Sätze in Aufgabe 1a als Muster, um über Ihren eigenen Tagesablauf zu schreiben.

2 Verbs + prepositions

Write in the missing prepositions.

1 Look _____ this photo.
2 Can you help me to look _____ my keys?
3 Tell children: *Don't talk _____ strangers!*
4 What are they talking _____ ?
5 Do you enjoy listening _____ opera?
6 I bought the flowers _____ the florist's.
7 I bought them _____ my mother on Mother's Day.

 49 **Say it right:** Listen and repeat the sentences.

3 Homophones
Homophones sind Wörter, die gleich klingen, aber unterschiedlich geschrieben werden. Ergänzen Sie die fehlenden Wörter.

1a Is this exercise _____ difficult?
1b I'm going _____ try it.
1c We have _____ teachers.

2a _____ an email to her.
2b Yes, that's _____ .

3a Do you often _____ jeans?
3b _____ are my keys?

4a _____ teacher is from the US.
4b Is _____ a café in your school?
4c _____ not here – they left 10 minutes ago.

 50 **Say it right:** Listen and repeat the sentences.

Phrases to learn: Keeping in touch

See you again in the next course.	*Wir sehen uns im nächsten Kurs wieder.*
Let's get together before the new term starts.	*Lasst uns uns treffen bevor das nächste Semester beginnt.*
Would you like my phone number?	*Hätten Sie gerne meine Telefonnummer?*
Should we exchange email addresses?	*Sollen wir unsere Mailadressen austauschen?*

 51 **Say it right:** Listen and repeat the sentences.

6 Topic | You

Write about ...

your family

your job (past or present)

your English course

your last holiday

a typical day

your plans for the future

And what's next?

Gut gemacht – jetzt haben Sie Ihren A1 Kurs abgeschlossen und damit die Niveaustufe A1 im Englischen erreicht. Denken Sie daran, dass Ihr Englisch nicht perfekt sein muss. Haben Sie keine Angst vor Fehlern und lassen Sie sich vor allem dadurch nicht vom Sprechen abhalten. Man versteht Sie auf alle Fälle, auch wenn Sie noch nicht 100%-ig perfekt sprechen.

Sehen Sie – ruhig mit Stolz – was Sie schon alles können:

- Sie haben gelernt über viele verschiedene Dinge zu sprechen, z.B. Ihre Hobbies und Interessen, Ihren Beruf, Ihre Heimatstadt, den letzten Urlaub, das Wetter etc.
- Sie können ein Formular auf Englisch ausfüllen, einkaufen gehen, die Uhrzeit angeben, nach dem Weg fragen, eine Einladung schreiben, eine kurze Präsentation auf Englisch geben und viele andere Alltagssituationen bewältigen.
- Sie können mit den passenden Zeitformen über Vergangenes, Gegenwärtiges und Zukünftiges sprechen.
- Auf den *Globetrotter*-Seiten haben Sie die notwendigen Redemittel an die Hand bekommen, um in beruflichen und touristischen Situationen zurechtzukommen.
- Und außerdem haben Sie viel Interessantes über kulturelle Unterschiede zwischen englischsprachigen Ländern und Deutschland erfahren.

Damit haben Sie schon eine Menge gelernt und sind bestens vorbereitet, um Ihre Englischkenntnisse und -fähigkeiten im nächsten Kurs erfolgreich auszubauen!

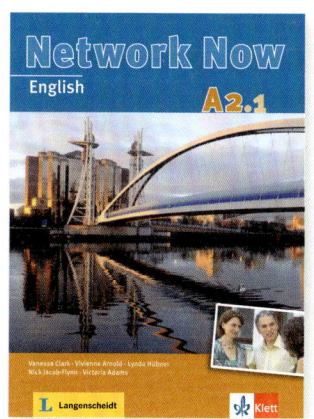

In Ihrem nächsten Kurs werden Sie mit *Network Now A2.1* weiterlernen – dem ersten Band der mittleren Niveaustufe.

- Sie werden z.B. lernen eine E-Mail auf Englisch zu schreiben, online für einen Flug einzuchecken, eine Unterkunft für Ihren Urlaub zu buchen, einen Termin zu vereinbaren und viele weitere Strategien an die Hand bekommen, damit Sie problemlos im Alltag und auf Reisen kommunizieren können.
- Dabei werden Sie auf viele Ihnen bereits vertraute Seiten stoßen wie z.B. *Now I can*, *Selfstudy*, *Reading*, *Now me*, *Globetrotter*, *Language and culture* und *Test yourself*.
- Und Sie können sich in jeder Unterrichtsstunde auf informative und unterhaltsame Texte freuen – lesen Sie z.B. über einen Mann, der ein Auto für 3 Millionen Euros verkauft hat; über einen Ladenbesitzer, der auf ungewöhnliche, aber sehr effektive Weise gegen lästigen Abfall vor seiner Ladentür kämpft und warum ein berühmter Professor eine Firma verklagt hat, die Toilettenpapier herstellt.

See you in the next course!

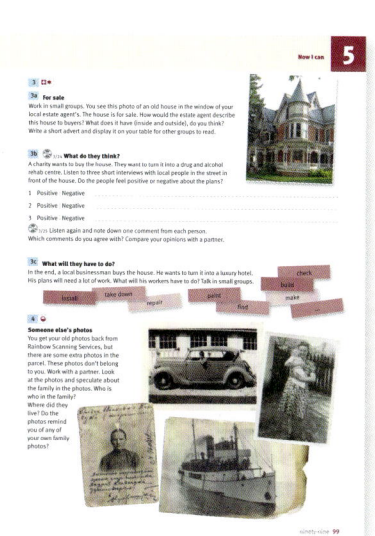

Key – Lösungsschlüssel

Unit 1

Step 1 (page 4 / 5)

1a Hi – I'm (Henry). / My name's (Henry).
(This is (Henry).)
Nice to meet you, (Henry).
★(Henry), good to see you again.

2a 1 Hello, 2 Pleased, 3 Nice, 4 How, 5 well, 6 introduce, 7 meet

2b 1 Hi - I'm (Lisa). 2 Nice to meet you. 3 Good to see you again. 5 Fine, thanks. 6 This is (Lisa).

2c 3 (Nice to meet you.)

3a 1 This, 2 Those, 3 These, 4 That

4 The doctor was the young man's mother.

Step 2 (page 6 / 7)

1a ☺☺ I love it. I think it's great. ☺ I like it. ☺ I think it's all right. I think it's OK. ☹ I don't like it very much. ☹☹ I can't stand it. I hate it.

1b 1 She likes tennis. 2 She likes playing tennis. 3 She doesn't like watching football. 4 She doesn't like swimming.

2a 1 ☺, 2 ☹, 3 ☺, 4 ☹, 5 ☺, 6 ☺

3a 2 your; 3 He, him; 4 her, her; 5 Its; 6 our, us; 7 your, you; 8 their, them

3b 1 My; 2 your; 3 me, you; 4 I, you; 5 We, you; 6 I, her

Step 3 (page 8)

2a 1f), 2a), 3b), 4h), 5g), 6e), 7c), 8d)

2b 1 Greece, 2 Switzerland, 3 Poland, 4 Austria, 5 Turkey, 6 The Czech Republic

Step 3 – Vocabulary from Unit 1 (page 9)

2a pen | hairbrush | passport | key | lipstick | newspaper | comb

4a 1 family name, 2 first name(s), 3 where you were born, 4 when you were born, 5 job

Topic (page 10 / 11)

1 1 Franz-Josef Strauß, 2 Konrad Adenauer, 3 W.A. Mozart, 4 John F. Kennedy (JFK), 5 Charles de Gaulle, 6 Leonardo da Vinci, 7 Václav Havel

2 1f), 2g), 3d), 4b), 5h), 6a), 7e), 8c)

3 1 Rom, 2 Venedig, 3 München, 4 Athen, 5 Köln, 6 Genf, 7 Mailand, 8 Wien

4 1g), 2d), 3f), 4c), 5e), 6a), 7l), 8j), 9h), 10k), 11b), 12i)

Unit 2

Step 1 (page 12 / 13)

1a It's … 1 twenty to one / twelve forty. 2 twenty-four minutes past six / six twenty-four / about twenty-five past six. 3 twenty-five to six / five thirty-five.

2a It's … 1 half past twelve. 2 twenty-five past four. 3 ten past seven. 4 quarter to three. 5 twenty to five. 6 five to eight.

2b 2 11.15 pm, quarter past eleven at night; 3 3.30 am, half past three in the morning; 4 9.35 pm, twenty-five to ten in the evening; 5 10.10 am, ten past ten in the morning; 6 2.20 pm, twenty past two in the afternoon

3a 1 Does he like hockey? 2 Yes, he does. / No, he doesn't. 3 He likes tennis but he doesn't like hockey.

3b 1 Do you like …? 2 I do … but my husband doesn't. 3 … does he enjoy? 4 He enjoys … but I think he prefers …, 5 Do you often go …? 6 No, we don't. He doesn't really like …!

4a 3a), 1b), 2c)

Step 2 (page 14 / 15)

1a 1b), 2e), 3c), 4a), 5d)

1c 1 drink, 2 drink, 3 drink, 4 drinking, 5 drink, 6 to drink

1d 1 idea, 2 love / like, 3 sounds, 4 Sorry

2a **IN** the morning, May, 1952, summer; **ON** Christmas Day, Wednesday, my birthday, February 1st; **AT** Christmas, 9.30, Easter, night

3a 1 How are you? 2 Who / How

4a 1 Whose, 2 How, 3 Who, 4 Which, 5 How, 6 Why

4b 1 from, 2 in, 3 for, 4 to, 5 in, 6 to, 7 about, 8 to

Step 3 (page 16)

1a 1 There was, there were; 2 there isn't, There was, there aren't; 3 There weren't, there is, there is; 4 There is, there was, There were

2c 1 She gets up at 6 o'clock every morning. 2 She always drinks coffee in the morning. 3 She doesn't have breakfast in the week. 4 She goes to work twice a week. 5 She usually leaves the house at 7.30 am. 6 She never has a winter holiday.

Step 3 – Vocabulary from Unit 2 (page 17)

1a **Across:** 1 fascinating, 3 boring, 6 pleased, 7 pretty; **Down:** 1 friendly, 2 awful, 4 different, 5 easy

2a 1 hotel, 2 shop, 3 hospital, 4 office, 5 factory, 6 restaurant

3a 1 cleaner, 2 chef, 3 doctor, 4 receptionist, 5 electrician, 6 retired

Key – Lösungsschlüssel

Topic (page 18 / 19)

1

3 1 They made their money in beer-brewing, banking and politics. 2 Arthur Guinness first started the brewing company. 3 He started it / the company in Dublin. 4 You can buy Guinness in 120 different countries. 5 Great Britain was the first country to import Guinness. 6 It was Sir Hugh Beaver's idea. 7 He was the managing director. 8 They published it / the first book in 1957. 9 Because it's the book which people steal most often from the library.

Unit 3

Step 1 (page 20 / 21)

1a 1 It's in Covent Garden. 2 He was a doctor. 3 He injured his foot. 4 They opened the first factory in Seeshaupt. 5 Because they were so comfortable. 6 He ordered boots for the Swiss Guard – and a pair for himself.

2a 1 1a Q: Where did they open (the first factory?) 1b Q: Was (the factory in Austria?) – A: (No, it) wasn't(, it) was (in Germany.) 1c Q: Did they open (a factory in Augsburg?) – A: (No,) they didn't(.) 1d Q: When did they open (the Seeshaupt factory?) 2 2a Q: Did the pope order (boots or shoes?) – A: He didn't order (shoes, he) ordered (boots.) 2b Q: (How) many did he order(?) 2c Q: Were (all the boot for him?) – A: (No,) they weren't(.) 2d Q: What colour were (the boots?)

3a 2 make, 3 meet, 4 buy, 5 take, 6 sell

3b 1 have | ~~had, was~~ | were; 2 have | ~~had, have~~ | had; 3 buy | ~~bought~~; 4 ~~buy~~ | bought, was | ~~were~~; 5 ~~was~~ | were

Step 2 (page 22 / 23)

1a 1 wet, 2 cold, 3 hot, 4 windy, 5 sunny, 6 foggy, 7 cloudy

1b 1 What's the weather like in your country? 2 Was the weather nice yesterday? 3 Which is your favourite season?

2a 1 What; 2 This; 3 looks, smells, tastes; 4 sounds

3a 1 ~~as~~ | when, 2 ~~Please~~. | You're welcome., 3 Where | ~~Who~~, 4 do | ~~make~~, 5 ~~for thirty years~~ | thirty years ago

4a 1 bought, 2 came, 3 drank, 4 ate, 5 got, 6 went, 7 had, 8 saw, 9 wore, 10 wrote

Step 3 (page 24)

1a 1 Would, 2 Would you, 3 Would you like, 4 Would you like to, 5 Would you like to go, 6 Would you like to go to

1b 1 love, 2 What, 3 about, 4 sorry

2a 1b), 2d), 3c), 4e), 5a)

2b 1 killed, 2 came, 3 landed, 4 took, 5 won, 6 wrote, 7 bought, 8 made, 9 died

Step 3 – Vocabulary from Unit 3 (page 25)

1a a) two, b) twelve, c) fifteen, d) ninety-eight, e) a / one hundred

1b a) thirty-first, b) twenty-second, c) third, d) thirtieth

2a bikini, blouse, dress, skirt

Topic (page 26 / 27)

1 1h), 2b), 3c), 4f), 5d), 6a), 7g), 8e)

4 1 Britain, 2 India, 3 the United States, 4 Japan, 5 Germany

Unit 4

Step 1 (page 28 / 29)

1a 1 eggs and baking items, 2 magazines, cards and newspapers, 3 flowers and gifts, 4 fruit and vegetables, 5 tinned food and drinks, 6 meat and fish, 7 checkouts

1b 1 next to; 2 on; 3 near; 4 between; 5 opposite; 6 in, on; 7 on, between

1c 1 Excuse, 2 there, 3 near, 4 is, 5 in, 6 exactly, 7 office, 8 next, 9 much, 10 welcome

2a 1 a, 2 an, 3 an, 4 a, 5 an, 6 a, 7 a, 8 an, 9 an, 10 a

2b 1 ~~a~~ | any; 2 ~~a~~ | any; 3 ~~any~~ | some; 4 ~~a~~ | some, ~~a~~ | some; 5 any | ~~some~~; 6 ~~any~~ | some; 7 a | ~~an~~

3a

S	P	O	S	Y	S	C	P	O	N
C	C	H	U	R	C	H	O	F	O
H	U	X	P	E	H	R	S	F	R
C	A	F	E	F	O	I	T	I	E
M	O	P	R	I	O	L	O	C	S
R	Y	U	M	P	L	Z	F	E	T
T	J	B	A	N	K	I	F	B	A
L	I	B	R	A	R	Y	I	L	U
C	C	K	K	W	U	T	C	O	R
Q	U	E	E	B	H	Z	E	C	A
A	H	O	T	E	L	O	I	K	N
E	V	O	S	R	J	O	P	S	T

fifty-three 53

Key – Lösungsschlüssel

3b 1 café, restaurant, hotels; 2 bank, post office; 3 office blocks; 4 supermarkets; 5 library, school; 6 zoo

4a 1b), 2h), 3e), 4g), 5a), 6d), 7f), 8c)

Step 2 (page 30 / 31)

1a 1 Excuse, 2 Can, 3 Could, 4 like, 5 much, 6 else, 7 all

1b 1c), 2f), 3a), 4d), 5e), 6b)

1c 1 How much are (the) potatoes / they? 2 Could / Can I have five kilos of potatoes, please? 3 That's all, thank you.

2a 1 much, 2 are, 3 cost, 4 each, 5 pence, 6 pounds

2b 1 twelve pence, 2 eight pounds, 3 forty pounds ninety-two, 4 fifty-two pounds

3a 1 ~~countable~~ | uncountable, 2 countable | ~~uncountable~~, 3 can | ~~can't~~

3b 1 many, 2 much, 3 much, 4 much, 5 many

4 Basket Ⓐ belongs to James. Basket Ⓑ belongs to Peter. Basket Ⓒ belongs to Paul. Basket Ⓓ belongs to Toby.

Step 3 (page 32)

1a 1 You can, 2 You don't have to, 3 You can, 4 You have to, 5 You can't, 6 You have to, 7 You can

2a 1 Great Britain, 2 United Kingdom, 3 United States of America, 4 European Union, 5 pound(s), 6 dollar(s)

3a 1T, 2T, 3F, 4F, 5F, 6T

Step 3 – Vocabulary from Unit 4 (page 33)

1a **to read:** book, magazine; **to eat:** chocolate, biscuits; **to drink:** champagne, wine; **to wear:** pullover, hat; **to play with:** game, teddy bear; **to use in the kitchen:** teapot, coffee pot; **to look at:** photo album, flowers

2a 1 cheese, 2 potatoes, 3 eggs, 4 bread, 5 meat, 6 onions, 7 chocolate, 8 yoghurt, 9 oranges, 10 coffee, 11 tea, 12 salami, 13 butter, 14 soup

3a 1 bottle, 2 packet, 3 kilo, 4 bag, 5 jar, 6 tin, 7 piece

Topic (page 34 / 35)

2 1 People buy more expensive items.
2 Because shoppers buy more when they use big carts.
3 The smell of bread, cake and cooked meats tempts shoppers (to buy spontaneously).
4 <u>Placing items that complement each other means a shopper buys two items, not just the one.</u> / <u>… – but that's at the opposite end of the store. So you have to walk through the store and you see more products.</u> / <u>But don't only compare the packets at eye-level, look on the lower shelves, too – that's where supermarkets often put their own, cheaper brands.</u> / <u>Snack items are near the checkout – shoppers want a reward.</u>

3 17–21 points: You enjoy looking around shops like some people enjoy looking around art galleries! Window shopping makes you nearly as happy as buying things. You love spending time and money in shops!
12–16 points: You are an organised shopper – you shop when you have to and you know what you want. You check for special offers but only buy them if it's what you need and the price is right.
7–11 points: You are an anti-shopper. You know your spending limits and you don't buy things you don't need. You would be happy if you never went into another shop!

Unit 5

Step 1 (page 36 / 37)

1a **Start of the call:** This is (Liz). Is that (Sam)? I'd like to ask about … How are you?
End of the call: Bye – see you next week. Thanks for phoning. It was nice to talk to you. I have to go now.

1b 1e), 2c), 3g), 4f), 5d), 6b), 7a)

1c A: this; B: How; A: can; B: sorry, moment; A: worry, later

2a 1 by plane, 2 by car, 3 by bike / bicycle, 4 on foot

2b 1 On foot. 2 By car. 3 By taxi. 4 By train. 5 By plane. 6 By bike.

2c 1 He travelled on 24th May. 2 He travelled from Gatwick Airport. 3 He travelled to Brighton. 4 No, it wasn't (it was for an adult). 5 The ticket was £8.30. 6 It was a single ticket. 7 It was a British ticket.

3a 1d), 2e), 3f), 4a), 5b), 6g), 7h), 8c)

4a 2 more comfortable than, 3 prettier than, 4 nicer than, 5 hotter than, 6 more popular than, 7 friendlier than, 8 more beautiful than, 9 dirtier than, 10 older than

4b 1 interesting; 2 busier; 3 older, older; 4 bigger; 5 more beautiful

Step 2 (page 38 / 39)

1a 1 most popular | ~~more popular~~; 2 ~~bigger~~ | biggest, than | ~~then~~; 3 busiest | ~~most busy~~, more | ~~most~~

1b 1 …, busiest; 2 …, most beautiful; 3 …, most difficult; 4 …, oldest; 5 …, most interesting; 6 …, biggest; 7 …, nicest

2a 1 Excuse, near; 2 Could, tell, way; 3 Where's, nearest

2b Excuse me, is there ... 1 a cash machine, 2 a bank, 3 a supermarket, 4 a cinema, 5 an Italian restaurant, 6 a station, 7 a shoe shop ... near here?

2c

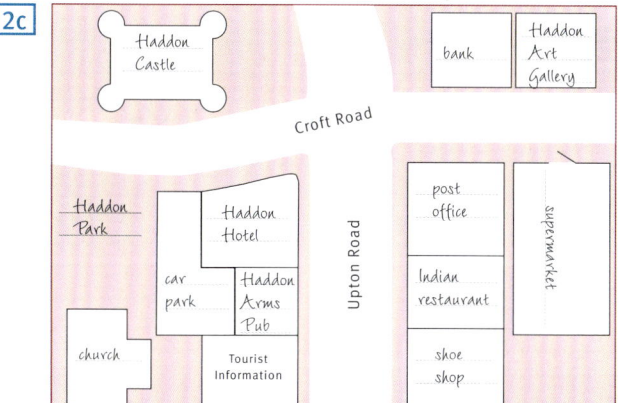

2d 1 Haddon Castle, 2 supermarket, 3 Haddon Hotel, 4 Haddon Art Gallery, 5 Indian restaurant

Step 3 (page 40)

1a 1 worst, worse, bad; 2 good, better, best

1b 1 the cheapest, 2 the most expensive, 3 the best, 4 the newest, 5 the most interesting, 6 the worst, 7 the biggest, 8 the busiest

2a 1 When, 2 Which, 3 Where, 4 How, 5 What, 6 How

2b 4a), 3b), 1c), 6d), 2e), 5f)

2c 1 When, 2 half past nine in the evening / 9.30 pm, 3 arrives, 4 How much is, 5 delays

Step 3 – Vocabulary from Unit 5 (page 41)

1a 1 It's three thirty / half past three. 2 It's June the twenty-first / the twenty-first of June. 3 The hotel has six floors. 4 It's / The cheapest single room is £46. 5 Breakfast is at seven thirty (half past seven) / from seven thirty (half past seven) till ten. 6 Her room number is a hundred and one. 7 The latest you can check out is at eleven forty-five / quarter to twelve.

2a 1 main road, zebra crossing; 2 crossroads, traffic lights, corner; 3 bridge, station

3a **bike:** c), f), i); **bus:** b), d), g); **plane:** a), e), g); **taxi:** b), d), h)

Topic (page 42 / 43)

2 1 Ham, 2 Sophie, 3 The bird, 4 Ham, 5 The bird, 6 Sophie

3 1c), 2c), 3b), 4a), 5b)

Unit 6

Step 1 (page 44 / 45)

1a 1 She's going to wash her hair. 2 They're going to bake muffins. 3 He's going to check emails. 4 I'm going to have / make / drink a cup of tea.

1b 1 She's isn't going to wash her hair. 2 They aren't going to bake muffins. 3 He isn't going to check emails. 4 I'm not going to have / make / drink a cup of tea.

1c 1 He's going to the supermarket later. 2 They're going to Paris in summer. 3 I'm going to work on Monday. 4 The children are going to school at eight o'clock.

1d 1 They're going to the cinema. 2 She's going to the bank. 3 He's going to the dentist's. 4 They're going to the theatre. 5 She's going to the hairdresser's. 6 They're going to the zoo. 7 She's going to the Indian restaurant.

1e I'm going to ... / I'm not going to ... 1 smoke, 2 watch, 3 do, 4 read, 5 write, 6 make

1f Mögliche Lösung: They're going to fly to London on June 19th. They're going to have a holiday in London. They're going to spend a week in London. They're going to fly with BA. They're going to travel economy class. ...

2a next week, tomorrow, in 2025, next year, the day after tomorrow, in two years' time, soon

3a 1e), 2b), 3c), 4d), 5a)

Step 2 (page 46 / 47)

1a 1 Are they going to do the next course after the holiday? 2 Is he going to have a holiday when the course ends? 3 Is the English course going to continue next term? 4 Are you going to stop learning English when this course ends? 5 Is she going to buy the A2 coursebook before the new course starts? 6 Are we going to meet in the holidays to practise English?

1b 3a), 1b), 6c), 4d), 2e), 5f)

3a 1 Yes, I am. / No, I'm not. 2 Yes, I do. / No, I don't. 3 Yes, I would. / No, I wouldn't. 4 Yes, I do. / No, I don't.

4a 1 soon, 2 forget, 3 See, 4 Have, 5 great, 6 Thank, 7 later, 8 Send

Step 3 (page 48)

1a 1c) I'd like to make an appointment for a check-up. 2a) Would Tuesday afternoon be OK for you? 3d) I'm sorry, I can't come on Tuesday. 4b) What about Friday morning? 5e) Yes, Friday is fine with me.

1b 1, 8, 6, 4, 7, 3, 2, 5

Key – Lösungsschlüssel

2a **Past:** 1 The lesson began at 7pm. 2 Did he speak a lot of English? 3 They didn't write a lot of emails. **Present:** 1 The lesson begins at 7pm. 2 Does he speak a lot of English? They don't write a lot of emails. **Future:** 1 The lesson is going to begin at 7 pm. 2 Is he going to speak a lot of English? 3 They aren't going to write a lot of emails.

Step 3 – Vocabulary from Unit 6 (page 49)

1a 1 First of all, she got up. Then she had a shower and got dressed. After that she ate breakfast and listened to the news. And finally she went to work.

2 First of all, she decided where to go. Then she bought tickets and found her passport. After that she booked a hotel. And finally she left for a holiday.

2 1 at, 2 for, 3 to, 4 about, 5 to, 6 from, 7 for

3 1a too, 1b to, 1c two; 2a Write, 2b right; 3a wear, 3b Where; 4a Their, 4b there, 4c They're

Acknowledgements – Bildnachweis

The material reproduced in this book has been taken from the following sources:

cover photolibrary.com (Britain on view); **4** Linda Rogers Association (Graham Round (Illustrator)), London; **5.1** Shutterstock (Gergely Attila), New York; **5.2** Shutterstock (Orfeev), New York; **6** Shutterstock (ostill), New York; **7** Shutterstock (sbarabu), New York; **9** Shutterstock (Gergely Attila), New York; **10.1** Shutterstock (Neftali), New York; **10.2** Shutterstock (catwalker), New York; **10.3** Shutterstock (Neftali), New York; **10.4** Shutterstock (Neftali), New York; **10.5** Shutterstock (catwalker), New York; **10.6** Shutterstock (catwalker), New York; **10.7** Shutterstock (catwalker), New York; **10.8** Shutterstock (rook76), New York; **11.1** Shutterstock (ekler), New York; **11.2** Shutterstock (natt), New York; **12.1** Shutterstock (Mapics), New York; **12.2** Shutterstock (Daryl Lang), New York; **12.3** Shutterstock (Brian King), New York; **14** Shutterstock (Gergely Attila), New York; **15.1** Shutterstock (Transia Design), New York; **15.2** Shutterstock (Rafal Olechowski), New York; **16** Shutterstock (TsipiLevin), New York; **17** Shutterstock (Gergely Attila), New York; **18.1** Shutterstock (pavalena), New York; **18.2** Shutterstock (caamalf), New York; **19** Shutterstock (Milosz_M), New York; **20** Shutterstock (Paul Cowan), New York; **21** Shutterstock (oculo), New York; **22.1** Shutterstock (Kuttly), New York; **22.2** Shutterstock (Eric Isselee), New York; **22.3** Shutterstock (Gtranquillity), New York; **22.4** Shutterstock (Natalia Klenova), New York; **22.5** Shutterstock (Nina Buday), New York; **23** Shutterstock (bikeriderlondon), New York; **24** Shutterstock (Ivan Negin), New York; **25** Shutterstock (Rashevskyi Viacheslav), New York; **26.1** Shutterstock (Olivier Le Moal), New York; **26.2** Shutterstock (grynold), New York; **27** Shutterstock (chlhii), New York; **28** Clipartseite.de; **31.1** Shutterstock (monticello), New York; **31.2** Shutterstock (Yelena Panyukova), New York; **31.3** Shutterstock (paul prescott), New York; **31.4** Shutterstock (cherries), New York; **32.1** Shutterstock (phipatbig), New York; **32.2** Shutterstock (phipatbig), New York; **32.3** Shutterstock (Radu Bercan), New York; **33.1** Shutterstock (agrino), New York; **33.2** Shutterstock (vector icons), New York; **34** Shutterstock (Stuart Miles), New York; **35** Shutterstock (snja), New York; **37** Shutterstock (Luca_Luppi), New York; **38** Shutterstock (Brian A Jackson), New York; **40** Shutterstock (Arena Photo UK), New York; **41.1** Dave Vaughan, München; **41.2** Shutterstock (stockshoppe), New York; **42.1** Shutterstock (Daniel Hebert), New York; **42.2** Shutterstock (Eric Isselee), New York; **42.3** Shutterstock (Erik Lam), New York; **43** Shutterstock (Claudio Divizia), New York; **44.1** Shutterstock (Konstantin Faraktinov), New York; **44.2** Shutterstock (matka_Wariatka), New York; **44.3** Shutterstock (bloomua), New York; **44.4** Shutterstock (caimacanul), New York; **46** Shutterstock (Zern Liew), New York; **47.1** Shutterstock (iQoncept), New York; **47.2** Shutterstock (nemlaza), New York; **48.1** Shutterstock (racorn), New York; **48.2** Shutterstock (M.Go), New York; **49** Shutterstock (PointaDesign), New York; **53** Shutterstock (pavalena), New York

We should be very grateful for any information which might assist us in tracing the copyright owners of sources we have been unable to acknowledge.